Contents

CHAPTER 10 Weight

CHAPTER 11 Picture Graphs and Bar Graphs

Math in Focus®
Singapore Math®
by Marshall Cavendish

Workbook

Consultant and Author
Dr. Fong Ho Kheong

Authors
Chelvi Ramakrishnan and Bernice Lau Pui Wah

U.S. Consultants
Dr. Richard Bisk, Andy Clark, and Patsy F. Kanter

Marshall Cavendish
Education

U.S. Distributor

Houghton
Mifflin
Harcourt

COMMON
CORE

© Copyright 2009, 2013 Edition Marshall Cavendish International (Singapore) Private Limited
© 2014 Marshall Cavendish Education Pte Ltd
(Formerly known as Marshall Cavendish International (Singapore) Private Limited)

Published by Marshall Cavendish Education
Times Centre, 1 New Industrial Road, Singapore 536196
Customer Service Hotline: (65) 6213 9444
US Office Tel: (1-914) 332 8888 | Fax: (1-914) 332 8882
E-mail: tmesales@mceducation.com
Website: www.mceducation.com

Distributed by
Houghton Mifflin Harcourt
222 Berkeley Street
Boston, MA 02116
Tel: 617-351-5000
Website: www.hmheducation.com/mathinfocus

First published 2009
2013 Edition

Math in Focus® Grade 1 Workbook B
ISBN 978-0-669-01325-2

Printed in Singapore

11 12 13 14   1401   18 17 16 15
4500524144   A B C D E

Mental Math Strategies

Calendar and Time

Numbers to 100

Addition and Subtraction to 100

CHAPTER 18 Multiplication and Division

CHAPTER 19 Money

BLANK

 Weight

Practice 1 Comparing Things

Circle your answer.

> **Example**
>
> Which is lighter?
>
>  watermelon   lemon

Which is heavier?

1.

2.

Fill in the blanks with *heavier than, lighter than* or *as heavy as*.

Example

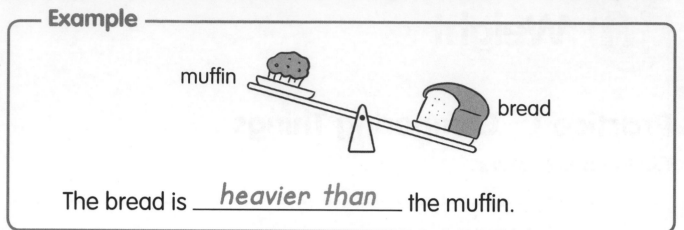

The bread is ___*heavier than*___ the muffin.

3.

toothbrush   cubes

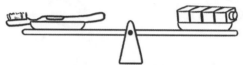

The toothbrush is _____ the cubes.

The cubes are _____ the toothbrush.

4.

bananas   fish

The fish is _____ the bananas.

The bananas are _____ the fish.

Name: _____   **Date:** _____

Fill in the blanks.

Example

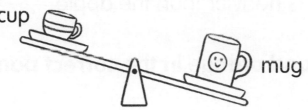

The ___*mug*___ is heavier than the ___*cup*___.

5.

The _____ is heavier than the _____.

The _____ are lighter than the _____.

6.

The _____ is heavier than the _____.

The _____ is lighter than the _____.

7. Mrs. Todd has an apple and an orange.
She puts them on a balance.
The orange is heavier than the apple.

Draw the apple and orange in the correct pans.

apple

orange

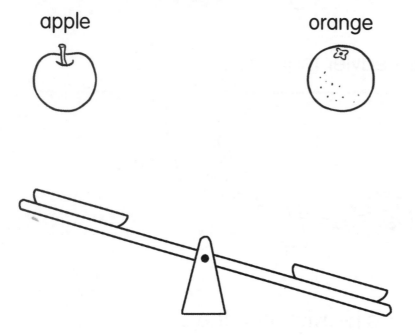

Guess which is heavier.
Color the heavier object.
Then check using a balance.
Circle the heavier object.

8.

My Guess		It Is	
orange	scissors	orange	scissors
book	a piece of paper	book	a piece of paper
a piece of paper	2 paper clips	a piece of paper	2 paper clips
orange	book	orange	book

9.   How many correct guesses did you make? _____

Look at the things.
Fill in the blanks.

feather   ostrich   egg

10. The _____ is the heaviest.

11. The _____ is the lightest.

Fill in the blanks.

tomato

carrot

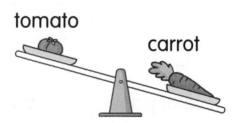

12. The _____ is lighter than the _____.

carrot

pumpkin

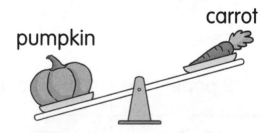

13. The _____ is heavier than the _____.

14. So, the pumpkin is heavier than the _____.

15. The _____ is the heaviest.

16. The _____ is the lightest.

Name: _____ Date: _____

Practice 2 Finding the Weight of Things

Fill in the blanks.

Example

clothes pins   paper ball

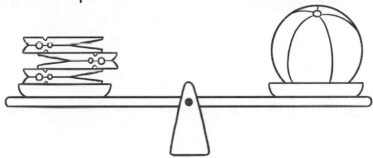

The weight of the paper ball is about ____3____ clothes pins.

1.

doll   toy bricks

The weight of the doll is about _____ toy bricks.

2.

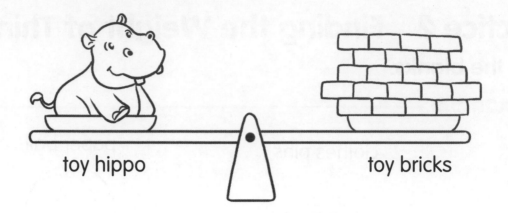

toy hippo   toy bricks

The weight of the toy hippo is about _____ toy bricks.

3.

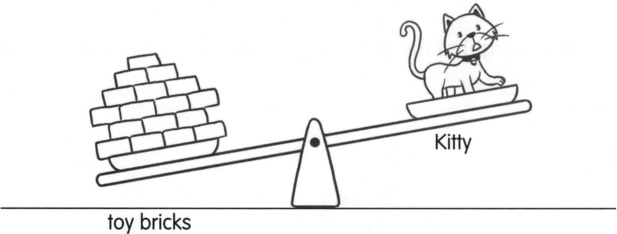

toy bricks   Kitty

The weight of Kitty is more than 15 toy bricks.

The weight of Kitty is about _____ toy bricks.

Name: _____   **Date:** _____

Look at the pictures
Then fill in the blanks.

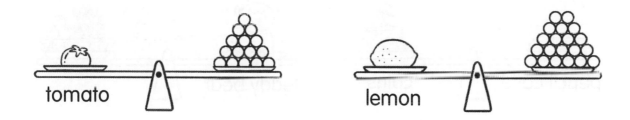

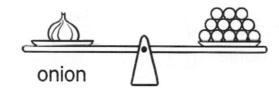

4.   The weight of the tomato is about _____ beads.

5.   The weight of the lemon is about _____ beads.

6.   The weight of the onion is about _____ beads.

7.   The tomato is heavier than the _____.

8.   The tomato is lighter than the _____.

9.   The _____ is the heaviest.

10. The _____ is the lightest.

**Look at the pictures.
Then fill in the blanks.**

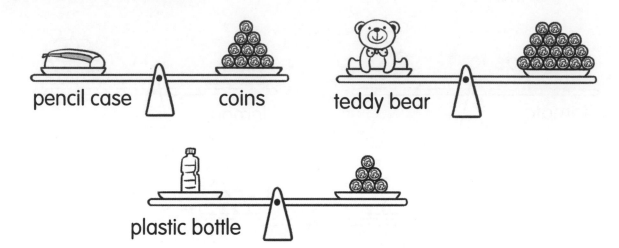

pencil case   coins   teddy bear

plastic bottle

11.   The weight of the pencil case is _____ coins.

12.   The weight of the plastic bottle is _____ coins.

13.   The weight of the teddy bear is _____ coins.

14.   The _____ is heavier than the plastic bottle.

15.   The _____ is lighter than the teddy bear.

16.   The pencil case is heavier than the _____.

17.   The _____ is lighter than the _____.

18.   The heaviest thing is the _____.

19.   The lightest thing is the _____.

Practice 3   Finding Weight in Units

Fill in the blanks.

Example

1 🪙 stands for 1 unit.

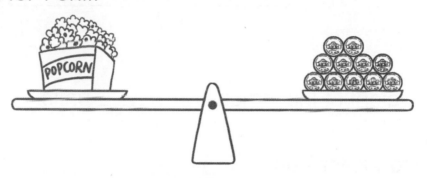

The weight of the box of popcorn is ___*11*___ units.

1.   1 ⬜ stands for 1 unit.

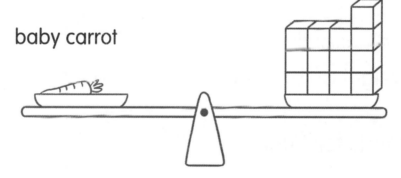

baby carrot

The weight of the baby carrot is _____ units.

2.   1 🔵 stands for 1 unit.

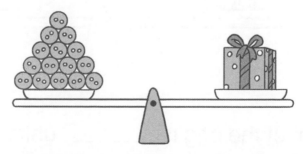

The weight of the gift is _____ units.

3. 1 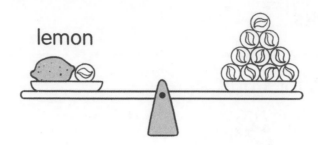 stands for 1 unit.

The weight of the lemon is _____ units.

4. 1 ⬚ stands for 1 unit.

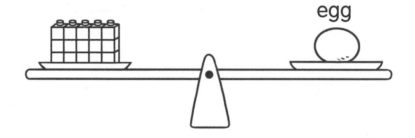

The weight of the egg is _____ units.

5. 1 🧷 stands for 1 unit.

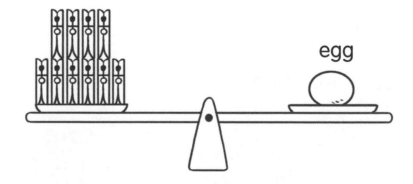

The weight of the egg is _____ units.

Name: _____   **Date:** _____

Fill in the blanks.

1 ⭐ stands for 1 unit.

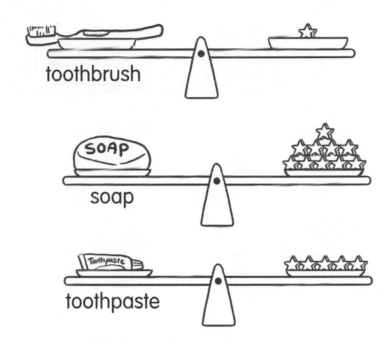

toothbrush

soap

toothpaste

6.   The weight of the toothbrush is _____ unit.

7.   The weight of the soap is _____ units.

8.   The weight of the toothpaste is _____ units.

9.   The _____ is lighter than the toothpaste.

10. The soap Is heavier than the _____.

11. The _____ is the heaviest.

12. The _____ is the lightest.

Fill in the blanks.

1 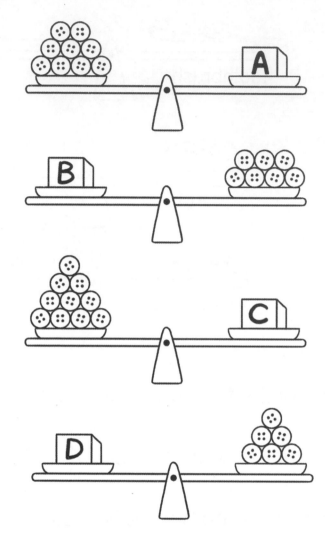 stands for 1 unit.

13. The weight of Box A is _____ units.

14. The weight of Box B is _____ units.

15. The weight of Box C is _____ units.

16. The weight of Box D is _____ units.

17. Box _____ is the heaviest.

18.   Box _____ is the lightest.

19.   Box _____ is heavier than Box D.

20.   Box _____ is lighter than Box A.

21.   Arrange the Boxes A to D in order from the heaviest to the lightest.

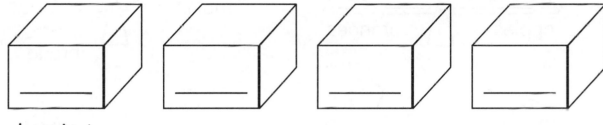

heaviest

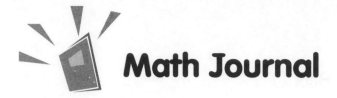

Math Journal

Look at the pictures.
1  stands for 1 unit.

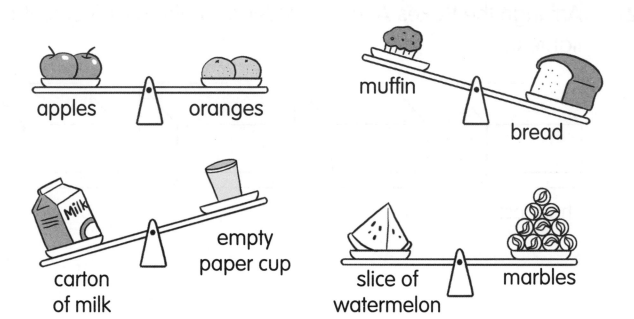

apples   oranges

muffin   bread

carton
of milk   empty
paper cup

slice of
watermelon   marbles

Write the correct answer.

1. The _____ are as heavy as the _____.

2. The _____ is heavier than the _____.

3. The _____ is lighter than the _____.

4. The slice of watermelon is _____ units.

Name: _____   **Date:** _____

Put On Your Thinking Cap!

Challenging Practice

Solve.

1. Box A has a weight of 6 beads.
   Box B is 2 beads heavier than Box A.
   Draw the beads for Box A and Box B.

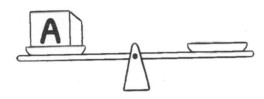   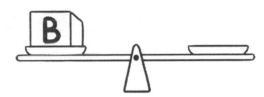

Look at the pictures.
Then answer the question.

2.

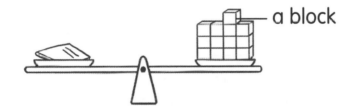   a block   a coin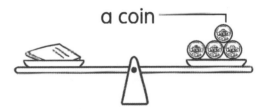

Which is heavier, a block or a coin? _____

Write *bananas* or *watermelon* in the blanks.

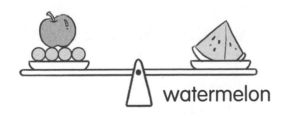   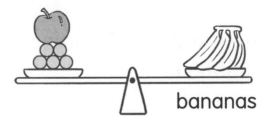

watermelon   bananas

3. The _____ are heavier than the _____.

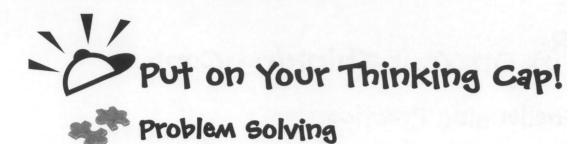

Put on Your Thinking Cap!

Problem Solving

Look at the plants.

1.

sunflower — cactus

sunflower — rose

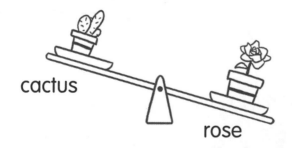

cactus — rose

Arrange the plants in order of their weight from the heaviest to the lightest.

_____   _____   _____

heaviest

Name: _____   **Date:** _____

Chapter Review/Test

Vocabulary

Choose the correct word.

weight
unit
heavy
as heavy as
lighter

1. The _____ of a thing is how heavy or light it is.

2. A _____ is the quantity used for measuring a thing.

3. A lion is a _____ animal.

4.

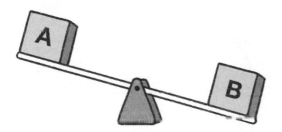

   Box A is _____ than Box B.

5.

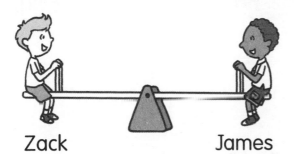

   Zack   James

   James is _____ Zack.

Concepts and Skills

Fill in the blanks.

6.

baby   boy

The _____ is heavier.

The _____ is lighter.

Check (✓) the heavier thing.

7.

8.

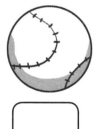

9.

10.

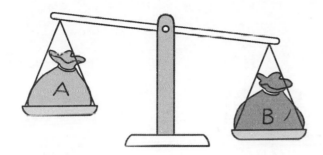

Bag A is _____ than Bag B.

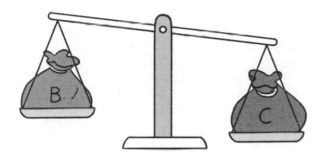

Bag B is _____ than Bag C.

So, Bag A is _____ than Bag C.

11.

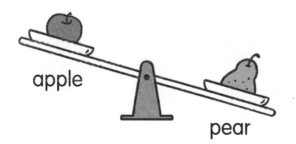

apple

pear

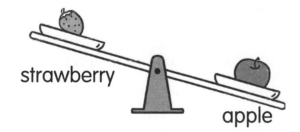

strawberry

apple

The _____ is the heaviest.

The _____ is the lightest.

1 ⬛ stands for 1 unit.

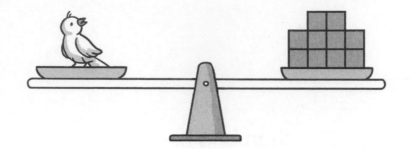

12. The weight of the bird is about _____ units.

1 🌀 stands for 1 unit.

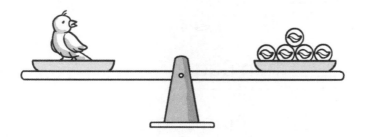

13. The weight of the same bird is about _____ units.

14. The number of units is different because _____.

_____.

Problem Solving
Solve.

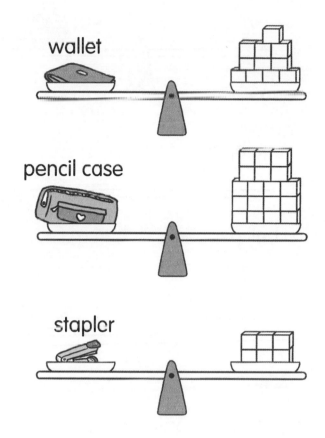

15.   The weight of the wallet is _____ 🔲.

16.   The weight of the pencil case is _____ 🔲.

17.   The weight of the stapler is _____ 🔲.

18.   Which is the heaviest? _____

19.   Which is the lightest? _____

20.   The _____ is heavier than the _____.

21.   The _____ is lighter than the _____.

1 ⚫ stands for 1 unit.

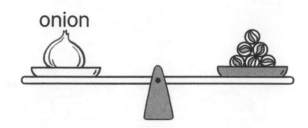

onion

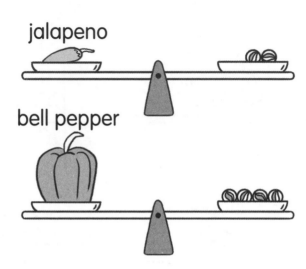

jalapeno

bell pepper

22. What is the weight of the onion? _____ units

23. What is the weight of the jalapeno? _____ units

24. What is the weight of the bell pepper? _____ units

25. Which is the heaviest? _____

26. Which is the lightest? _____

27. Arrange the things in order from the lightest to the heaviest.

_____, _____, _____
lightest

CHAPTER 11 Picture Graphs and Bar Graphs

Practice 1   Simple Picture Graphs

Daniel draws a picture graph of his friends' birth months.

Daniel's Friends' Birth Months

January	February	March	April

Use the graph to answer the questions.

1.   How many friends are born in January?   _____

2.   In which month are most of his friends born?   _____

Look at the picture graph.
Then fill in the blanks.

This picture graph shows the flowers in Shana's garden.

Flowers in Shana's Garden

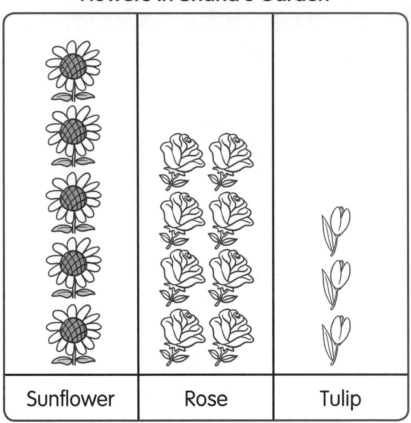

3. There are _____ sunflowers.

4. There are _____ roses.

5. There are _____ tulips.

6. There are _____ more roses than tulips.

7. There are _____ fewer tulips than sunflowers.

8. There are _____ flowers in all.

Look at the picture graph.
Then fill in the blanks.

This picture graph shows all the toys in Annie's toy box.

Toys in Annie's Toy Box

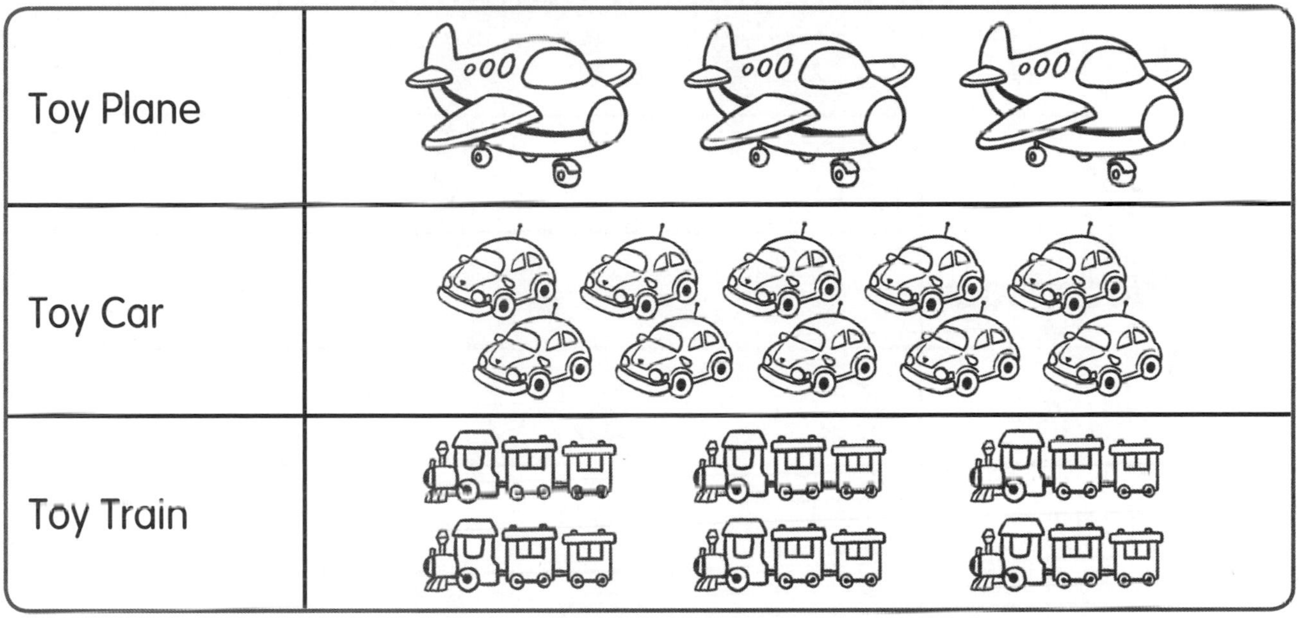

Toy Plane	
Toy Car	
Toy Train	

9. There are _____ toy planes in Annie's box.

10. There are _____ toy cars.

11. There are _____ toy trains.

12. The number of _____ is the greatest.

13. The number of _____ is the least.

14. Annie has _____ toys in all.

15. There are _____ more toy cars than toy trains.

16. There are 7 fewer _____ than _____.

Look at the picture graph.
Then fill in the blanks.

This picture graph shows the coins Barry saves in a week.

Barry's Savings

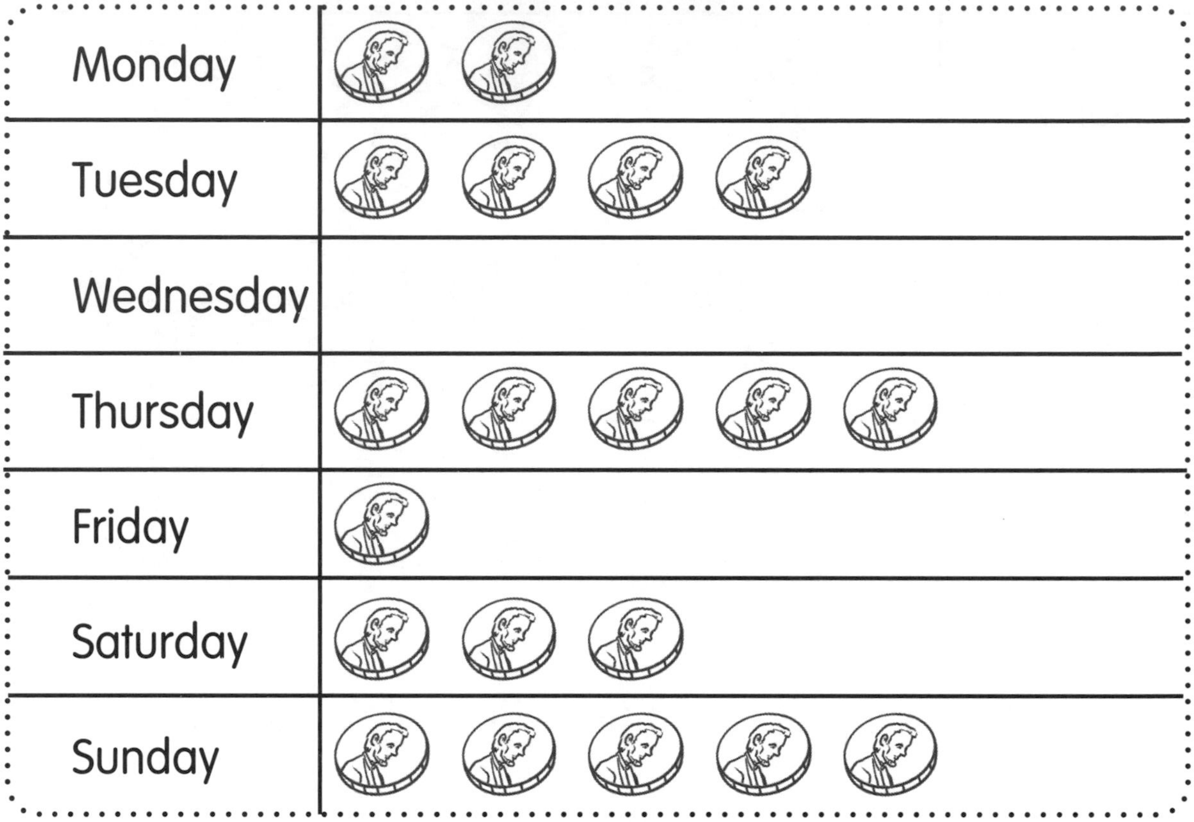

Monday	🪙 🪙
Tuesday	🪙 🪙 🪙 🪙
Wednesday	
Thursday	🪙 🪙 🪙 🪙 🪙
Friday	🪙
Saturday	🪙 🪙 🪙
Sunday	🪙 🪙 🪙 🪙 🪙

17. How many coins does Barry save on Monday? _____ coins

18. How many coins does he save on Tuesday? _____ coins

19. Barry saves 1 coin on Friday.

He saves _____ more coins on Saturday.

20. How many coins in all does he save from Thursday to

Saturday? _____ coins

21. He does not save on _____.

Name: _____   Date: _____

Practice 2   More Picture Graphs

Alonso has a coin.

Every time he tosses the coin, he gets heads 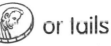 or tails .

Alonso tosses the coin many times.

This is what he gets:

Count the tosses.
Color a ☐ for each toss.

Alonso's Tosses

🪙									
🪙									

Each ☐ stands for 1 toss.

1.   comes up _____ times.

2. 🪙 comes up _____ times.

3. Color the side that comes up more times. 🪙 🪙

4. 🪙 comes up _____ more times than 🪙 .

Every student in Grade 1 has a pet.
The picture shows their pets.

Count the pets and complete the picture graph.

Grade 1's Pets

5.

Hamster	Goldfish	Dog	Cat	Rabbit	Bird

Each △ stands for 1 pet.

Fill in the blanks.

6. The most popular pet is the _____.

7. There are _____ hamsters.

8. There are _____ more cats than birds.

9. There are 4 fewer _____ than _____.

10. The number of _____ is the least.

11. The number of _____ is the greatest.

12. There are equal numbers of _____

    and _____.

Look at the picture graph.
Then fill in the blanks.

Monica goes to the zoo.
She makes a picture graph that shows the animals she sees.

Animals in the Zoo

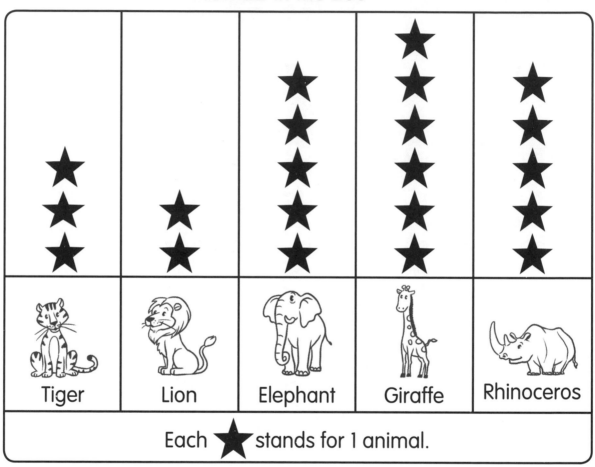

Each ★ stands for 1 animal.

13. Monica sees _____ tigers.

14. She also sees _____ giraffes.

15. She sees the most _____.

16. She sees the fewest _____.

17. There are _____ more rhinoceroses than lions.

18. There are _____ fewer tigers than elephants.

Name: _____   **Date:** _____

Look at the picture graph.
Then fill in the blanks.

This picture graph shows how a group of children goes to school.

Ways of Going to School

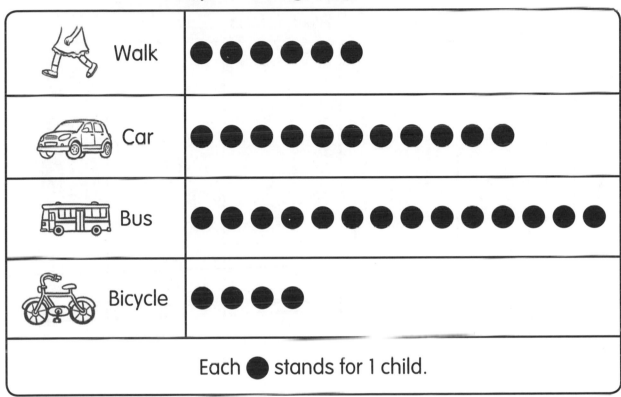

Each ● stands for 1 child.

19. How many children walk to school? _____

20. How many children go to school by bus? _____

21. How do most of the children go to school? _____

22. The fewest children go to school by _____.

23. More children walk to school than ride a bicycle.

How many more? _____

24. Fewer children go to school by car than by bus.

How many fewer? _____

**Look at the picture graph.
Then fill in the blanks.**

Jason invites his friends to a party.
This picture graph shows the fruit juices they drink.

Fruit Juices

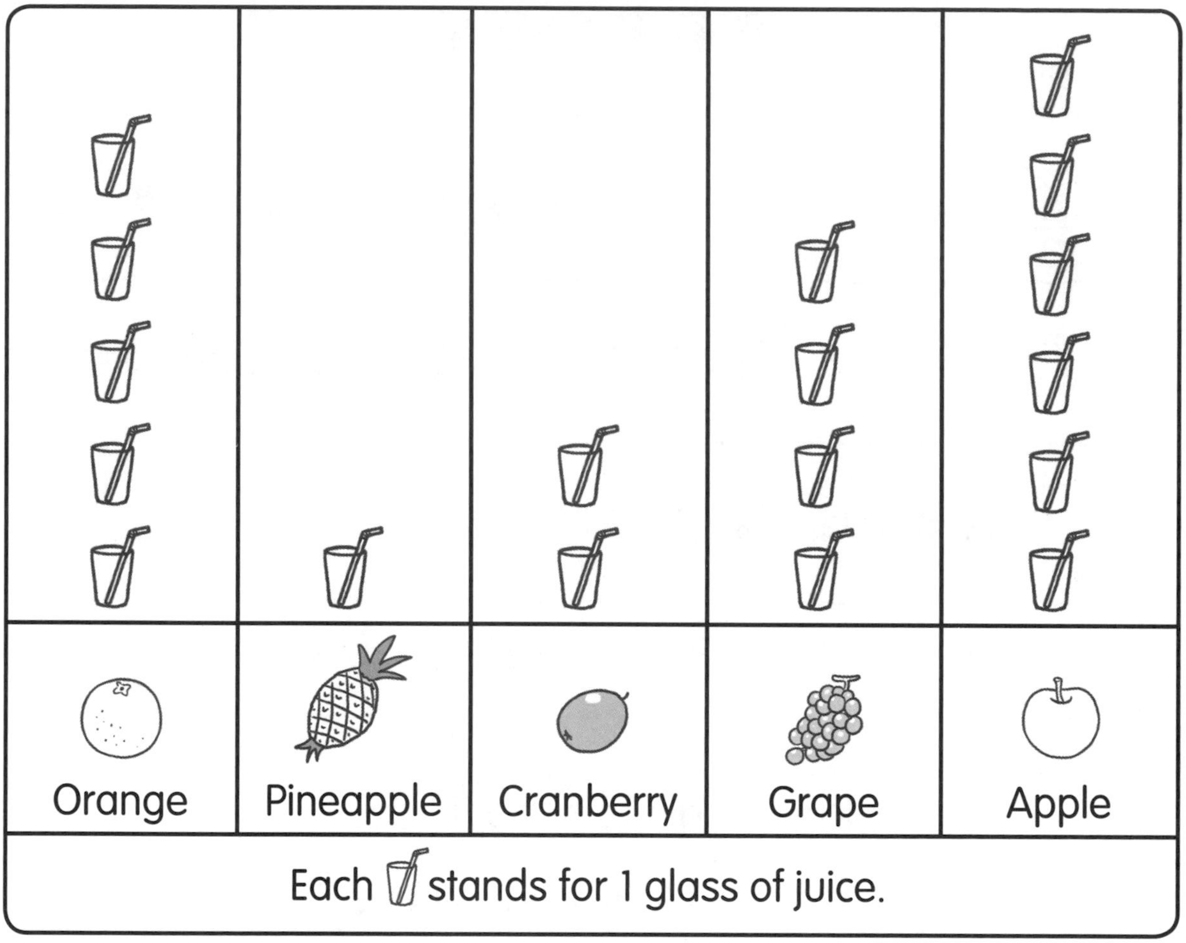

Orange	Pineapple	Cranberry	Grape	Apple

Each 🥤 stands for 1 glass of juice.

25. The children drink _____ glasses of cranberry juice.

26. What is the most popular juice? _____

27. They drink fewer glasses of pineapple juice
than orange juice.
How many fewer? _____

28. How many types of juices do they drink? _____

Practice 3   Tally Charts and Bar Graphs

There are some spoons, forks, and knives on the table.

Complete the tally chart.
Then answer the questions.

Silverware	Tally	Number
Spoon	ⵑⵑⵑ	5
Fork		
Knife		

1.   How many spoons are there? _____

2.   How many knives are there? _____

3.   There are 2 more _____ than spoons.

4.   How many fewer knives than forks are there? _____

Kelly bought balloons for her party.
The tally chart shows the different colors of balloons she bought.
Complete the tally chart.
Then fill in the blanks.

5.

Balloons	Tally	Number
Red	~~////~~ /	
Blue	~~////~~ ////	
Yellow	~~////~~ ~~////~~ ~~////~~	

6. Kelly bought _____ red balloons.

7. She bought _____ blue balloons.

8. Kelly bought _____ more yellow balloons than blue balloons.

9. She bought 9 fewer _____ balloons than _____ balloons.

Abby bought some seed packages.
The tally chart shows the different kinds of seeds she bought.
Complete the tally chart.

10.

Seed Packages	Tally	Number
Cucumber	~~////~~ //	
Pumpkin	///	
Sunflower	~~////~~	

Make a bar graph.

11.

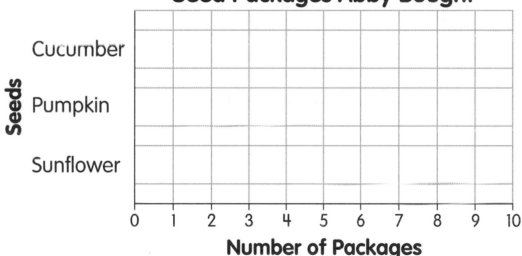

Seed Packages Abby Bought

Answer the questions.

12. How many packages of sunflower seeds did she buy?_____

13. How many more packages of cucumber seeds
than pumpkin seeds did she buy? _____

14. How many packages of seeds did she buy in all? _____

15. She bought 2 more packages of _____ seeds
than sunflower seeds.

Math Journal

Keep a record of how many books you read this week.
Include the books you read in class and those your teacher or
your family reads to you.
Draw 📖 to represent 1 book.

Number of Books I Read this Week

Sunday	Monday	Tuesday	Wednesday	Thursday	Friday	Saturday

Each 📖 stands for 1 book.

Look at your graph.
Write sentences about the number of books you have read.
You may use the words below.

more than	less than	most	fewest

_____

_____

_____

Name: _____   Date: _____

Put on Your Thinking Cap!

Challenging Practice

Team A, Team B, and Team C play a game.
The graph shows the number of points each child
on Team A scores.

Answer the questions.

Points for Team A

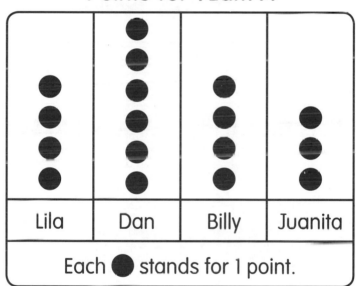

| Lila | Dan | Billy | Juanita |

Each ● stands for 1 point.

1. How many points did Team A score in all? _____

2. Team B scores 7 points fewer than Team A.
    How many points does Team B score? _____

3. Team A scores 3 points fewer than Team C.
    How many points does Team C score? _____

Tina and her friends, Eva and Pedro, brought
some crackers to school.
The tally chart shows the number of crackers each child brought.

Complete the tally chart.

4.

Children	Tally	Number of Crackers
Tina	~~////~~ //	
Eva	///	
Pedro	~~////~~	

Make a bar graph.

5.

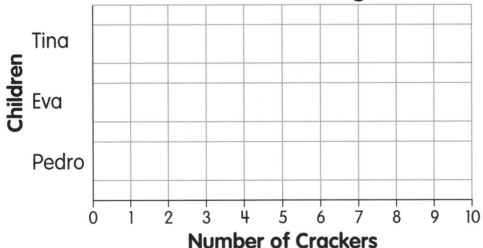

Crackers the Children Brought to School

6. How many crackers did Pedro bring? _____

7. How many more crackers did Tina bring than Eva? _____

8. How many crackers did the children bring in all? _____

9. Tina brought _____ more crackers than Pedro.

 # Put on Your Thinking Cap!

Problem Solving

The Art Club sold boxes of cards to three families along the same street.

Cards Sold by The Art Club

| Anderson | Bailey | Diaz |

Each ● stands for 1 box of cards.

Fill in the blanks.

1. The Bailey family bought _____ boxes of cards.

2. The _____ family bought the fewest boxes of cards.

3. The _____ family bought the most boxes of cards.

4. The Anderson family bought _____ fewer boxes of cards fewer than the Bailey family.

5. The families bought _____ boxes of cards in all.

6. Make a bar graph.

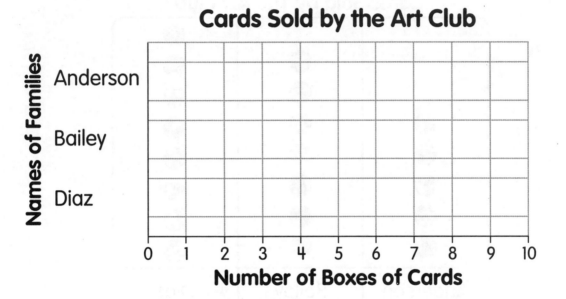

Chapter Review/Test

Vocabulary

Choose the correct word.

more
_____
fewer
_____
bar graph

1.   A _____ uses bars and a scale to show data.

Children at the Library

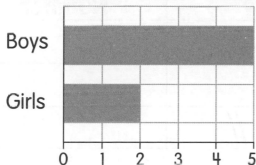

2.   There are _____ girls than boys.

3.   There are _____ boys than girls.

Concepts and Skills

The tally chart shows some children's favorite musical instruments.

Favorite Instruments	Tally	Number
Piano	~~HHH~~ ////	9
Guitar	~~HHH~~ ~~HHH~~ //	12
Drum	~~HHH~~ /	6

4.   _____ is the most popular musical instrument.

5.   _____ is the favorite musical instrument of the fewest children.

Problem Solving

A recycling project was carried out in a class.
Some children brought bottles for recycling.
The tally chart shows the number of bottles each child brought.

Complete the tally chart.

6.

Children	Tally	Number
Jay	~~IIII~~ ~~IIII~~	
Madison	III	
Kimberly	~~IIII~~ II	

Make a bar graph.

7.

Fill in the blanks.

8. How many bottles did Kimberly bring? _____

9. _____ brought the fewest bottles.

12 Numbers to 40

Practice 1   Counting to 40

First make tens, then count on.
Fill in the missing numbers.

┌─ **Example** ──────────────────────────────────────┐

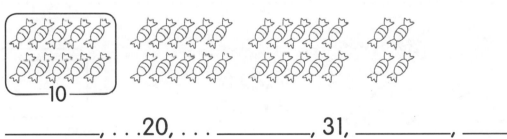

<u> 10 </u>, . . . <u> 20 </u>, <u> 21 </u>, <u> 22 </u>, <u> 23 </u>

└──┘

1.

_____, . . .20, . . . _____, 31, _____, _____,

_____

2.

10, . . . _____, . . . _____, _____, _____,

33, _____, _____, 36

Circle groups of 10.
Then count and write the numbers.

3.

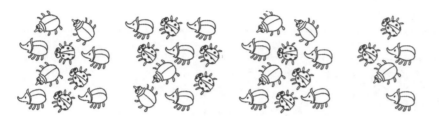 

....

4.

....

5.

....

6.

....

7.

Name: _____ Date: _____

Count the 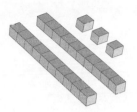s and write the numbers.

8.

_____

9.

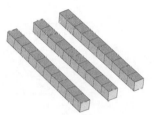

_____

10.

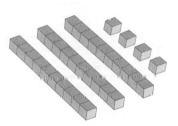

_____

11.

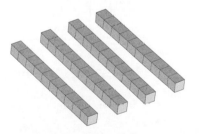

_____

Write the numbers.

12. twenty-five _____

13. thirty-nine _____

14. thirty-two _____

15. twenty-nine _____

Write the numbers in words.

16. 21 _____

17. 37 _____

18. 22 _____

19. 40 _____

20. 35 _____

21. 31 _____

Fill in the missing numbers.

22. 20 + 3 = _____

23. 8 + 30 = _____

24. _____ + 9 = 39

25. 30 and 5 make _____.

26. 7 and 20 make _____.

27. _____ and 2 make 32.

28. _____ and 8 make 28.

29. _____ and 6 make 36.

Practice 2   Place Value

Fill in the missing numbers.

1.

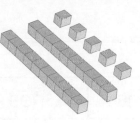

25 = _____ tens _____ ones

2.

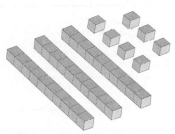

37 = _____ tens _____ ones

Look at each place-value chart.
Write the number it shows.

3.

Tens	Ones

4.

Tens	Ones

Count in tens and ones.
Fill in the missing numbers in the place-value charts and blanks.

Example

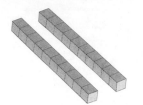

Tens	Ones
2	3

23 = ____2____ tens ____3____ ones

20 + 3 = ____23____

5.

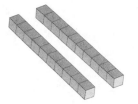

Tens	Ones

26 = _____ tens _____ ones

20 + 6 = _____

6.

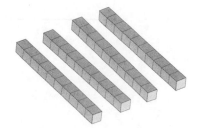

Tens	Ones

40 = _____ tens _____ ones

40 + 0 = _____

Practice 3   Comparing, Ordering, and Patterns

Find the missing numbers.

23	24	25	26	27	28	29	30	31	32	33	34	35	36	37	38	39	40

┌─ **Example** ───┐

1 more than 23 is ___24___.

1 less than 35 is ___34___.

└──┘

1.   1 more than 29 is _____.   **2.**   2 more than 19 is _____.

3.   2 more than 26 is _____.   **4.**   2 less than 31 is _____.

5.   3 more than 27 is _____.   **6.**   3 more than 36 is _____.

7.   3 less than 25 is _____.   **8.**   3 less than 40 is _____.

9.   _____ is 2 more than 27.   **10.**   _____ is 2 less than 26.

11.   _____ is 3 more than 30.   **12.**   _____ is 3 less than 30.

13.   _____ is 2 more than 35.   **14.**   _____ is 2 less than 35.

Count the |s in each set.
Fill in the blanks.

15.

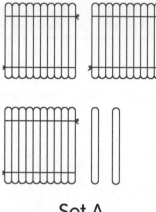

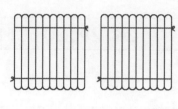

Set A   Set B

Which set has more? Set _____.

Which number is greater?

_____ is greater than _____.

16.

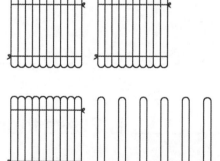

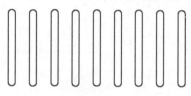

Set A   Set B

Which set has fewer? Set _____.

Which number is less?

_____ is less than _____.

Circle the greater number.

17.   32 or 23

18.   37 or 39

19.   19 or 21

20.   15 or 25

Circle the number that is less.

21.   32 or 28

22.   38 or 40

Compare the numbers.
Then fill in the blanks.

23.   _____ is the least.

24.   _____ is the greatest.

Order the numbers from least to greatest.

25.

_____, _____, _____
least

**Compare the numbers.
Then fill in the blanks.**

(23)   (38)   (35)   (27)

26.   _____ is less than 27.

27.   _____ is greater than 35.

28.   35 is greater than _____ and _____ but

       less than _____.

29.   The least number is _____.

30.   The greatest number is _____.

**Compare the numbers.
Then fill in the blanks.**

(40)   (24)   (39)   (26)

31.   _____ is 2 more than 24.

32.   _____ is 1 less than 40.

33.   _____ is less than 39 but greater than 24.

34.   The least number is _____.

35.   The greatest number is _____.

© Marshall Cavendish International (Singapore) Private Limited.

Complete each number pattern.

36. 18, 19, _____, 21, _____, 23, _____

37. 30, 31, 32, _____, _____, 35, _____

38. _____, _____, 30, 31, _____ 33, 34

39. 33, _____, 31, _____, _____, 28, 27

40. 30, 32, _____, _____, 38, _____

41. 27, _____, _____, _____, 19, 17, 15

42. _____, 23, 26, 29, _____, 35

43. 33, _____, _____, 24, 21, _____

44. _____, 10, _____, 30, 40

Solve.

45. Kim's ball falls into a number machine.
Which ball is it?

Write the missing number in the ◯.

Put on Your Thinking Cap!

Challenging Practice

Fill in the blanks.

Wayne has four cards.
Each card has a number on it.

2 1 3 0

1. Use two cards to form the least number.
    Do not begin with 0.

    _____

2. Use two cards to form the greatest number.

    _____

3. Use two cards to form a number less than 30.
    Do not begin with 0.

    _____

4. Use two cards to form a number greater than 25.

    _____

There is more than one correct
answer for Exercises 3 and 4.

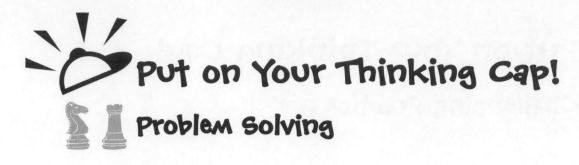

Put on Your Thinking Cap!

Problem Solving

Fill in the blanks.

Jan uses tiles to make shapes that form a pattern.

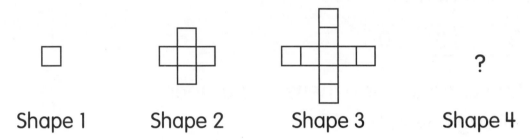

Shape 1   Shape 2   Shape 3   Shape 4

1. Draw Shape 4.

2. Jan needs _____ more tiles to make Shape 4.

3. Complete the table.

Shape Number	1	2	3	4	5
Number of Tiles	1	5	9		

4. Complete the number pattern.

1, 5, 9, _____, _____, _____

Chapter Review/Test

Vocabulary

Match.

1.

27 •   • thirty-eight

36 •   • forty

24 •   • twenty-seven

38 •   • twenty-four

40 •   • thirty-six

Concepts and Skills

Count to find how many.

2.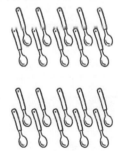

3.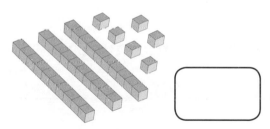

Write the numbers.

4.   twenty-four   _____   **5.**   thirty   _____

Write the number that is greater.

6.   ㉕ ⑰   _____   **7.**   ㉖ ㉙   _____

Write the number that is less.

8. (10) (29) _____

9. (38) (33) _____

Compare the numbers.
Then fill in the blanks.

/16\   /9\   /21\   /35\

10. Which number is greatest? _____

11. Which number is least? _____

Order the numbers from greatest to least.

12. _____, _____, _____, _____

    greatest

Complete the number pattern.

13. 17, 20, 23, _____, _____, 32

Fill in the blanks.

14. 2 less than 25 is _____.

15. _____ is 3 more than 18.

16. 24 = _____ tens 4 ones

17. 18 = 1 ten _____ ones

Name: _____ Date: _____

CHAPTER 13

Addition and Subtraction to 40

Practice 1 Addition Without Regrouping

Add by counting on.

Example

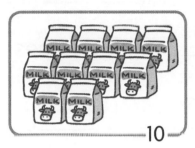  

—10— —10—

$20 + 3 =$ ___23___

1.

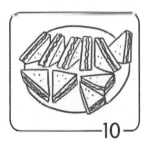  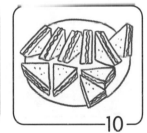 

—10— —10— —10—

$30 + 5 =$ _____

2.

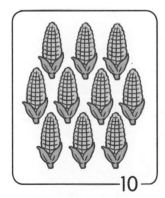 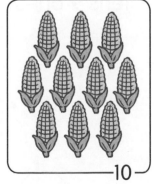 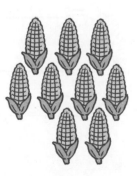

—10— —10—

$20 + 9 =$ _____

3.

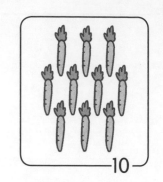 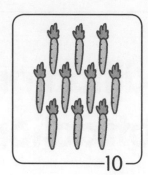 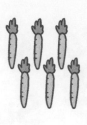

30 + 6 = _____

Fill in the missing numbers.

> **Example**
>
> 25 + 4 = ___2___ tens ___5___ ones + 4 ones
>
> = ___2___ tens 9 ones
>
> (20) (5) = ___29___

4.   32 + 6 = _____ tens _____ ones + 6 ones

= 3 tens _____ ones

= _____

5.   37 + 2 = _____ tens _____ ones + 2 ones

= _____ tens 9 ones

= _____

6.   16 + 2 = _____

7.   24 + 3 = _____

Complete each place-value chart.
Then add.

Example

	Tens	Ones
	2	5
+		2
	2	7

	Tens	Ones
25	‖	▢▢▢ ▢▢
2		▢▢

8.

	Tens	Ones
	2	7
+		2

	Tens	Ones
27	‖	
2		▢▢

9.

	Tens	Ones
	2	5
+	1	0

	Tens	Ones
25		▢▢▢ ▢▢
10		

Complete the place-value chart.
Then add.

10.

Tens	Ones
1	4
+ 2	3

	Tens	Ones
14		
23		

Add.

11.
```
    2  5
 +     4
_____
```

12.
```
       2
 +  2  6
_____
```

13.
```
    2  0
 +  2  0
_____
```

14.
```
    4  0
 +  2  4
_____
```

15. 25 + 12 = _____

16. 14 + 24 = _____

Practice 2   Addition with Regrouping

Fill in the missing numbers.

┌─ **Example** ───┐

$23 + 9 = $ _____2_____ tens _____3_____ ones + _____9_____ ones

$= $ _____2_____ tens _____12_____ ones

$= $ _____32_____

└───┘

1. $37 + 3 = $ _____ tens _____ ones + _____ ones

$= $ _____ tens _____ ones

$= $ _____

2. $25 + 8 = $ _____ tens _____ ones + _____ ones

$= $ _____ tens _____ ones

$= $ _____

3. $26 + 6 = $ _____ tens _____ ones + _____ ones

$= $ _____ tens _____ ones

$= $ _____

Fill in the missing numbers.

4.   5 + 29 = _____ ones + _____ tens _____ ones

          = _____ tens _____ ones

          = _____

5.   19 + 21 = _____ ten _____ ones + _____ tens _____ one

          = _____ tens _____ ones

          = _____

Add.

6.   1 8
       +   5
       _____

7.   2 4
       +   9
       _____

8.   5
       + 2 6
       _____

9.   1 6
       +   7
       _____

10.   1 6
       + 1 4
       _____

11.   2 5
       + 1 5
       _____

Fill in the missing numbers.

12.   18 + 7 = _____

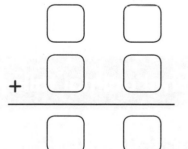

13.   21 + 9 = _____

14.   6 + 15 = _____

15.   8 + 32 = _____

16.   17 + 16 = _____

17.   13 + 19 = _____

Add.
Then solve the riddle.

18. $14 + 7 = \underline{\quad 21 \quad}$ **A**

19. $26 + 8 = \underline{\qquad}$ **I**

20. $29 + 6 = \underline{\qquad}$ **E**

21. $23 + 9 = \underline{\qquad}$ **N**

22. $33 + 7 = \underline{\qquad}$ **R**

23. $18 + 22 = \underline{\qquad}$ **R**

24. $6 + 24 = \underline{\qquad}$ **D**

25. $17 + 18 = \underline{\qquad}$ **E**

What animal falls from the clouds on a rainy day?

Match the letters to the answers below to find out.

☐	A	☐	☐	–	☐	☐	☐	☐
40	21	34	32		30	35	35	40

Practice 3 Subtraction Without Regrouping

Subtract by counting back.

Example

24 – 2 = _____22_____

24, 23, 22

1. 27 – 6 = _____

2. 35 – 4 = _____

3. 38 – 8 = _____

4. 24 – 3 = _____

5. 39 – 4 = _____

6. 39 – 9 = _____

Fill in the missing numbers.

Example

37 – 4 = _____3_____ tens 7 ones – _____4_____ ones

= _____3_____ tens 3 ones

= _____33_____

7. 38 – 3 = _____ tens _____ ones – 3 ones

= 3 tens _____ ones

= _____

Fill in the missing numbers.

8. 26 – 4 = _____ tens 6 ones – _____ ones

   = _____ tens 2 ones

   = _____

Subtract.

9.

Tens	Ones
1	6
–	2

10.

Tens	Ones
2	8
–	4

11.

Tens	Ones
3	5
–	2

12.

Tens	Ones
3	6
–	6

13.

Tens	Ones
4	0
– 2	0

14.

Tens	Ones
2	3
– 1	0

15.

Tens	Ones
3	6
– 1	1

16.

Tens	Ones
3	4
– 1	4

Fill in the missing numbers.

17. 29 – 26 = _____

Tens	Ones
⬜	⬜
– ⬜	⬜
⬜	⬜

18. 38 – 10 = _____

Tens	Ones
⬜	⬜
– ⬜	⬜
⬜	⬜

19. 31 – 20 = _____

Tens	Ones
⬜	⬜
– ⬜	⬜
⬜	⬜

20. 27 – 17 = _____

Tens	Ones
⬜	⬜
– ⬜	⬜
⬜	⬜

21. 36 – 5 = _____

Tens	Ones
⬜	⬜
– ⬜	⬜
⬜	⬜

22. 38 – 8 = _____

Tens	Ones
⬜	⬜
– ⬜	⬜
⬜	⬜

23. Joel puts a ball into a number machine.
Which ball is it?
Write the correct number in the ●.

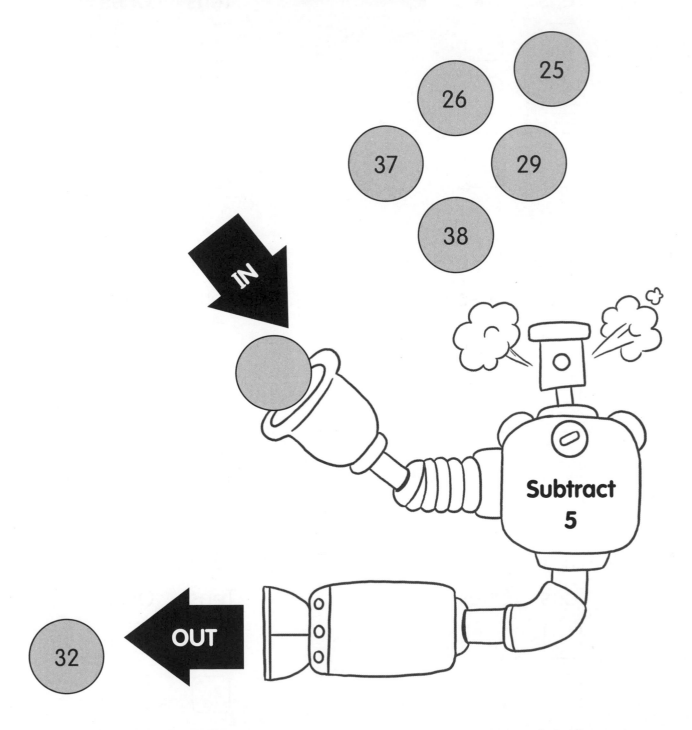

Practice 4   Subtraction with Regrouping

Regroup.

1.   27 = 1 ten _____ ones

2.   15 = 0 tens _____ ones

3.   30 = 2 tens _____ ones

Subtract.

4.
```
   2  3
-     6
_____
```

5.
```
   2  4
-     8
_____
```

6.
```
   3  3
-     5
_____
```

7.
```
   3  6
-     9
_____
```

8.
```
   2  5
-  1  6
_____
```

9.
```
   2  0
-  1  8
_____
```

Fill in the missing numbers.

10. 21 – 5 = _____

11. 36 – 7 = _____

12. 25 – 18 = _____

13. 31 – 18 = _____

14. 32 – 14 = _____

15. 30 – 17 = _____

Name: _____   Date: _____

Subtract.
Then solve the riddle.

16. $38 - 9 =$ ___29___   **W**

17. $30 - 18 =$ _____   **E**

18. $32 - 5 =$ _____   **S**

19. $35 - 8 =$ _____   **S**

20. $27 - 7 =$ _____   **A**

21. $34 - 19 =$ _____   **A**

How do you cut the sea?

Match the letters to the answers below to find out.

WITH A ⬜ ⬜ ⬜ - ⬜ ⬜ ⬜W⬜
‾27‾ ‾12‾ ‾20‾   ‾27‾ ‾15‾ ‾29‾

Natasha drops a ball into each number machine.
Write the missing numbers in the blanks to show what happens to each ball.

22.

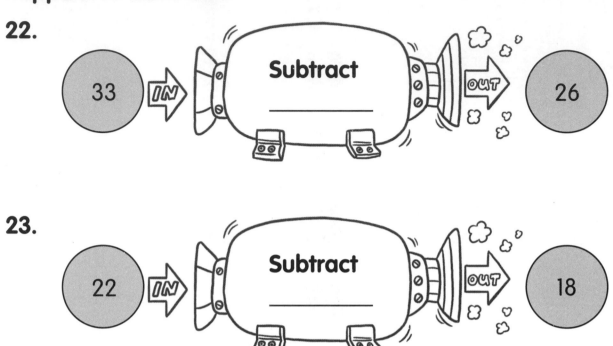

23.

Practice 5   Adding Three Numbers

Add.

1.

$4 + 5 + 6 =$ _____

2.

$8 + 7 + 7 =$ _____

3.

$6 + 9 + 8 =$ _____

4.

$5 + 4 + 8 =$ _____

Make ten.
Then add.

Example

$6 + 3 + 7 =$ ___16___

$6 + 10 = 16$

10

5. $5 + 8 + 5 =$ _____

Make 10 first.

6. $8 + 9 + 2 =$ _____

7. $9 + 7 + 2 =$ _____

8. $9 + 4 + 4 =$ _____

9. $2 + 9 + 5 =$ _____

Practice 6   Real-World Problems: Addition and Subtraction

Solve.

1.   Lynn has 12 trophies.
     Geeta has 5 more trophies than Lynn.
     How many trophies does Geeta have?

     Geeta has _____ trophies.

2.   Rima buys 15 stickers.
     Susie buys 7 fewer stickers than Rima.
     How many stickers does Susie buy?

     Susie buys _____ stickers.

Solve.

3.　Tara has 14 toy cars.
　　She has 9 more toy cars than Carlos.
　　How many toy cars does Carlos have?

　　Carlos has _____ toy cars.

4.　Aaron makes 6 friendship bracelets.
　　He makes 5 fewer friendship bracelets than Kate.
　　How many friendship bracelets does Kate make?

　　Kate makes _____ friendship bracelets.

Solve.

5. Michelle has 18 snowballs.
Miguel has 14 snowballs.
How many more snowballs does Michelle have?

Michelle has _____ more snowballs.

6. Rose buys 17 hairclips.
Sarah buys 13 more hairclips than Rose.
How many hairclips does Sarah buy?

Sarah buys _____ hairclips.

7. Tess has 22 walnuts.
She has 13 more walnuts than Chris.
How many walnuts does Chris have?

Chris has _____ walnuts.

8. Ashley makes 36 muffins.
Janice makes 17 muffins.
How many more muffins does Ashley make?

Ashley makes _____ more muffins.

Put on Your Thinking Cap!

Challenging Practice

Fill in the circles with numbers.

1.   Each ○—○—○ must make 8.

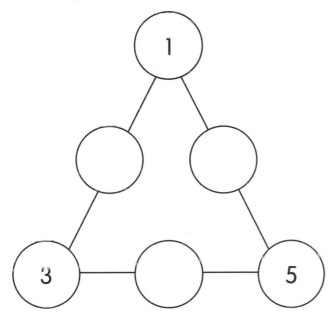

2.   Each ○—○—○ must make 10.

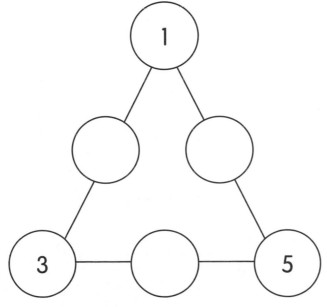

3. Luis places a ball into the number machine below. What happens to the number on the ball?

Fill in the missing numbers.

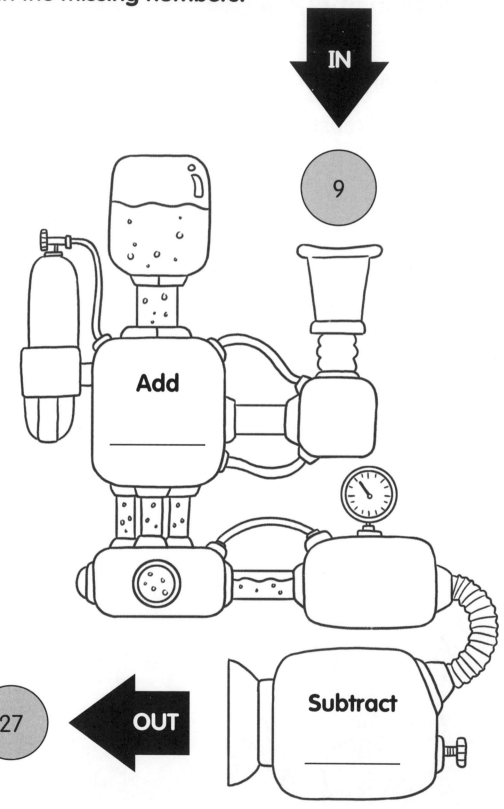

4. Luis places another ball into the number machine below. What happens to the number on the ball?

Fill in the missing numbers.

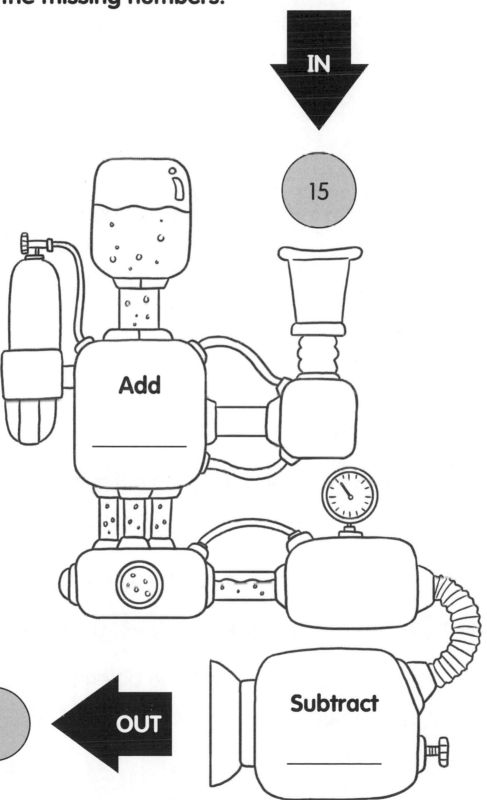

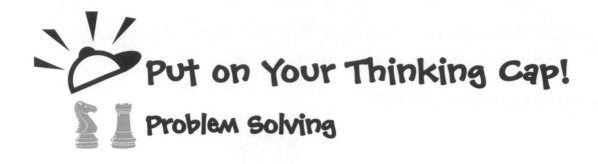

Put on Your Thinking Cap!

Problem Solving

Dawn, Jamal and Nate go to an amusement park.

Fun Rides

Roller Coaster	10 tokens
Bumper Car	7 tokens
Flying Elephant	6 tokens
Merry-Go-Round	5 tokens

They buy tokens.
Then they go for rides.
Which rides do they take?

Circle the correct rides.

1. Dawn uses 15 tokens to go on two different rides.

   Roller Coaster   Bumper Car   Flying Elephant   Merry-Go-Round

2. Jamal uses 12 tokens to go on two different rides.

   Roller Coaster   Bumper Car   Flying Elephant   Merry-Go-Round

3. Nate uses 21 tokens to go on three different rides.

   Roller Coaster   Bumper Car   Flying Elephant   Merry-Go-Round

Chapter Review/Test
Vocabulary
Choose the correct word.

1. You _____ from the greater number when you subtract.

2. You can _____ 13 ones into 1 ten 3 ones.

3. You can add two numbers using the _____ method.

4. A _____ can be used to add numbers.

regroup
counting on
count back
place-value chart

Concepts and Skills
Add or subtract.

5. 32 + 7 = _____

6. 18 + 19 = _____

7. 27 – 3 = _____

8. 36 – 18 = _____

9. 4 + 8 + 6 = _____

10. 9 + 8 + 5 = _____

Problem Solving

Solve.

11. Nicole blows up 30 balloons for a class party.
    Michael blows up 4 fewer balloons than Nicole.
    How many balloons does Michael blow up?

    Michael blows up _____ balloons.

12. Ryan has 23 bookmarks.
    He has 5 fewer bookmarks than Ivy.
    How many bookmarks does Ivy have?

    Ivy has _____ bookmarks.

Cumulative Review

for Chapters 10 to 13

Concepts and Skills

Fill in the blanks.
Write *heavier than, lighter than,* or *as heavy as.*

doll

book   ball   book

1. The book is _____ the ball.

2. The doll is _____ the book.

3. The ball is _____ the doll.

Fill in the blanks.

4. 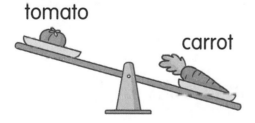 tomato carrot

 pineapple

The _____ is lighter than the carrot.

The _____ is heavier than the carrot.

So, the tomato is lighter than the pineapple.

The picture graph shows the number of cars and trucks in a parking lot.

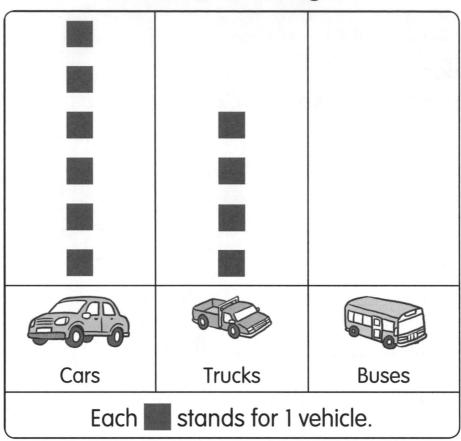

Vehicles in a Parking Lot

Cars

Trucks

Buses

Each ■ stands for 1 vehicle.

Fill in the blanks.

5. There are _____ more cars than trucks.

6. There are _____ cars and trucks in all.

7. There are 2 fewer buses than cars.
    Draw ■ to show the number of buses.

8. Some cars leave the parking lot.
    The number of cars and trucks are now the same.

    _____ cars leave the parking lot.

Complete the tally chart using the data from the picture graph.

9.

Kinds of Vehicles	Tally	Number
Cars	⫩⫩⫩⫩ |	
Trucks	||||	
Buses		

Make a bar graph using the data from the tally chart.

10.

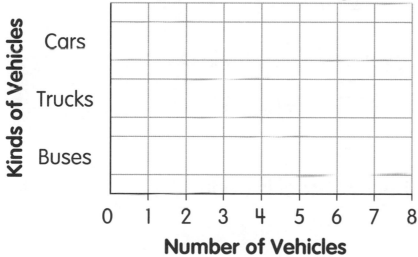

Vehicles in a Parking Lot

Fill in the blanks.

1 ○ stands for 1 unit.

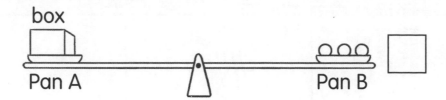

11. The weight of the box is _____ units.

12. Add 1 marble to Pan A.
Draw ↓ or ↑ in the ☐ to show if Pan B goes up or down.

Fill in the blanks.

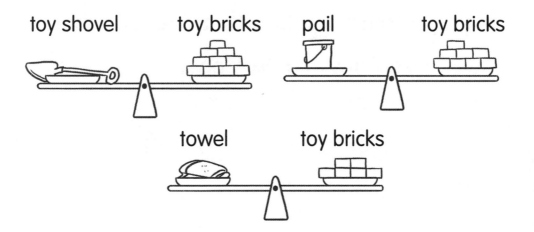

13. The weight of the toy shovel is about _____ toy bricks.

14. Order the objects from heaviest to lightest.

_____   _____   _____
heaviest

First make tens.
Then count on.
Fill in the missing numbers.

15.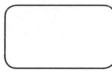

16.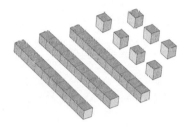

Write the number.

17. twenty-five _____

18. thirty _____

Write the number in words.

19. 37 _____

20. 40 _____

Fill in the missing numbers.

21. 7 + 20 = _____

22. _____ + 10 = 36

Find the missing numbers.

23.

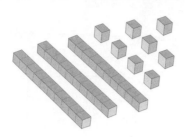

38 = _____ tens _____ ones

Look at the place-value chart.
Write the number it shows.

24.

Tens	Ones
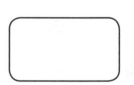

25.

Tens	Ones

Name: _____ **Date:** _____

Circle the greater number.

26. 25 or 17

27. 26 or 29

Circle the number that is less.

28. 10 or 29

29. 38 or 33

Compare the numbers.
Then fill in the blanks.

16   9   21   35

30. _____ is the least.

31. _____ is the greatest.

32. _____ is less than 35 but greater than 16.

33. Order the numbers from the least to greatest.

_____, _____, _____, _____

    least

Complete each number pattern.

34. 17, 20, 23, _____, _____, 32

35. 28, _____, 36, 40

Fill in the blanks.

36. 2 less than 25 is _____.

37. _____ is 3 more than 18.

38. 24 = _____ tens 4 ones

39. 18 = 1 ten _____ ones

Add or subtract.

40. 21 + 7 = _____

41. 24 + 10 = _____

42. 27 − 3 = _____

43. 38 − 15 = _____

44. 6 + 3 + 7 = _____

45. 9 + 8 + 5 = _____

46.
```
    2 3
  + 1 6
  ─────
```

47.
```
    2 9
  + 1 1
  ─────
```

48.
```
    1 4
  + 1 7
  ─────
```

49.
```
    1 8
  + 1 7
  ─────
```

50.
```
    3 6
  − 2 4
  ─────
```

51.
```
    3 6
  − 1 8
  ─────
```

52.
```
    2 1
  − 1 7
  ─────
```

53.
```
    3 2
  − 1 5
  ─────
```

Problem Solving

Solve.

54. Jamal has 20 stamps.
Michelle has 4 fewer stamps than Jamal.
How many stamps does Michelle have?

Michelle has _____ stamps.

55. Nate blows up 30 balloons for his birthday party.
Nate blows up 6 fewer balloons than Miguel.
How many balloons does Miguel blow up?

Miguel blows up _____ balloons.

Mental Math Strategies

Practice 1   Mental Addition

Add mentally.
First add the ones.
Then add the ones to the tens.

┌─ **Example** ─────────────────────────────┐

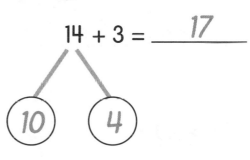

$14 + 3 =$ _____17_____

└───┘

1. $15 + 2 =$ _____

2. $12 + 4 =$ _____

3. $35 + 1 =$ _____

4. $23 + 5 =$ _____

5. $22 + 7 =$ _____

6. $31 + 8 =$ _____

7. $6 + 32 =$ _____

8. $5 + 34 =$ _____

Add mentally.
First add the tens.
Then add the tens to the ones.

Example

$13 + 10 = \underline{\quad 23 \quad}$

3   10

---

9. $18 + 10 = \underline{\qquad}$

10. $11 + 20 = \underline{\qquad}$

11. $12 + 10 = \underline{\qquad}$

12. $14 + 20 = \underline{\qquad}$

13. $16 + 10 = \underline{\qquad}$

14. $20 + 19 = \underline{\qquad}$

15. $10 + 17 = \underline{\qquad}$

16. $20 + 13 = \underline{\qquad}$

17. $10 + 14 = \underline{\qquad}$

18. $20 + 16 = \underline{\qquad}$

Add mentally.
Use doubles facts.

┌─ **Example** ───┐

$6 + 7 =$ ___*13*___

6 + 7 is double 6 plus 1.

└──┘

19. $4 + 5 =$ _____   **20.** $7 + 8 =$ _____

21. $5 + 6 =$ _____   **22.** $8 + 9 =$ _____

Solve mentally.
Fill in the blanks.

23.

I have 24 stickers.
I want 5 more.

Emily

Book Shop

How many stickers will Emily have?   _____

Solve mentally.
Fill in the blanks.

24.

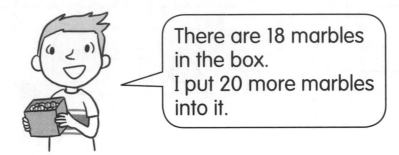

There are 18 marbles in the box.
I put 20 more marbles into it.

How many marbles are there in the box now? _____

25.

I bake 11 pecan muffins and 6 oat muffins.

Baker Ross

How many muffins does Baker Ross bake in all? _____

Practice 2   Mental Subtraction

Subtract mentally.
Think of addition.

1. $8 - 5 =$ _____

2. $9 - 6 =$ _____

3. $11 - 3 =$ _____

4. $13 - 7 =$ _____

5. $15 - 6 =$ _____

6. $12 - 8 =$ _____

Subtract mentally.
First subtract the ones.
Then add the ones to the tens.

┌─ **Example** ─────────────────────────────┐

$(27) - 3 =$ ___*24*___

(20) (7)

└───┘

7. $28 - 4 =$ _____

8. $29 - 5 =$ _____

9. $27 - 6 =$ _____

10. $37 - 2 =$ _____

11. $38 - 8 =$ _____

12. $36 - 6 =$ _____

Subtract mentally.
First subtract the tens.
Then add the tens to the ones.

> **Example**
>
>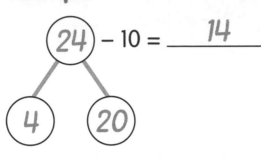
>
> $24 - 10 = \underline{\quad 14 \quad}$

13. $22 - 10 = \underline{\hspace{2cm}}$

14. $23 - 20 = \underline{\hspace{2cm}}$

15. $35 - 30 = \underline{\hspace{2cm}}$

16. $36 - 20 = \underline{\hspace{2cm}}$

Solve mentally.
Fill in the blanks.

17.

I have 16 fish.
9 of them swim away.

How many fish are left? _____

18.

There are 29 apples
and 10 pears in the
basket.

How many more apples than pears are there? _____

Name: _____ Date: _____

Put On Your Thinking Cap!

 Challenging Practice

You can use a telephone dial to find the value of a word.

> **Example**
>
> YES = 9 + 3 + 7 = 19

1. Name a three-letter word with a value of 14. _____

2. Find a word that has the same value as BOAT. _____

3. Think of a four-letter word.
   Find its value.
   Ask your friend to guess the word.

My word has a value of 20. Guess the word.

   _____

   _____

   _____

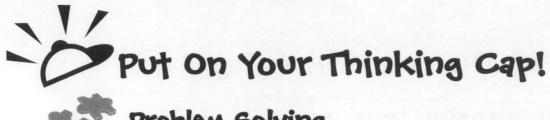 

There are 6 bicycles and tricycles
at Sunshine Day Care Center.
There are 16 wheels in all.
How many bicycles are there?

Draw a picture to help you.

Chapter Review/Test

Vocabulary

Choose the correct word.

1. To help you subtract _____, think of addition.

2. 4 + 4 = 8 is a _____.

doubles fact

mentally

Concepts and Skills

Add mentally.

3. 25 + 4 = _____

4. 33 + 4 = _____

5. 10 + 28 = _____

6. 15 + 20 = _____

7. 6 + 7 = _____

8. 4 + 7 = _____

Subtract mentally.
Think of addition.

9. 8 − 6 = _____

10. 9 − 7 = _____

11. 16 − 7 = _____

12. 18 − 9 = _____

13. 15 − 8 = _____

14. 14 − 7 = _____

Subtract mentally.

15. 15 – 4 = _____

16. 38 – 6 = _____

17. 21 – 10 = _____

18. 37 – 20 = _____

Problem Solving

Fill in the blanks.

19.

There were 27 stamps.
I lost 4 of them.

How many stamps are left? _____

20. 13 children are on a school bus.
6 more children get on the bus.
How many children are on the bus? _____

15 Calendar and Time

Practice 1   Using a Calendar

Fill in the blanks.

1.   How many days are in one week?

_____

Write the days of the week.

2.   The first day is _____.

3.   The third day is _____.

4.   The fifth day Is _____.

5.   The last day is _____.

6.   Which is your favorite day of the week?

_____

Every week begins on a Sunday.

Color or circle.

Color the third month of the year gray.

January	February	March
April	May	June
July	August	September
October	November	December

7. Color the month that it is now red.

8. Color the month of your birthday yellow.

9. Color the ninth month of the year green.

10. Circle the month that has 28 days using blue.

11. Circle the months that have only 30 days using purple.

January	February	March
April	May	June
July	August	September
October	November	December

2010

OCTOBER						
Sunday	Monday	Tuesday	Wednesday	Thursday	Friday	Saturday
					1	2
3	4	5	6	7	8	9
10	11	12	13	14	15	16
17	18	19	20	21	22	23
24	25	26	27	28	29	30
31						

Fill in the blanks.
Use the calendar to help you.

12. The name of the month is _____.

13. _____ is the day just before Wednesday.

14. There are _____ days in this month.

15. _____ is the day between Wednesday and Friday.

16. The date of the second Monday is _____.

17. The day of the week just after October 22, 2010 is

_____.

Match the picture to the season.

18.

- summer
- spring
- winter
- fall

Fill in the blanks.

Think about the seasons.
In what seasons are these holidays?

19. New Year's Day _____

20. Thanksgiving _____

21. Independence Day _____

Name: _____

Date: _____

Practice 2   Telling Time to the Hour

Match the clock to the time.

1.

   ●   ● 12 o'clock

   ●   ● 8 o'clock

   ●   ● 9 o'clock

   ●   ● 3 o'clock

   ●   ● 4 o'clock

Fill in the blanks.

This is what Roberta does on Monday.

Example

She brushes her teeth at ___7 o'clock___.

2.

Her math class starts at _____.

3.

She has lunch at _____.

4.

She plays with her friends at _____.

5.

Roberta practices piano at _____.

6.

She has her dinner at _____.

Name: _____   Date: _____

7.

She does her homework at _____.

8.

She goes to bed at _____.

Color the clock faces that show the correct time.

9. 3 o'clock ....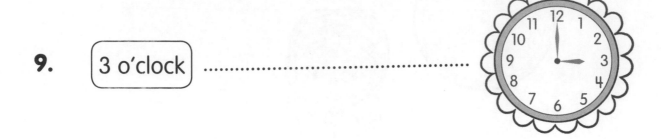

10. 9 o'clock ....

11. 12 o'clock ....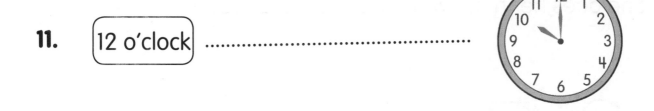

12. 5 o'clock ....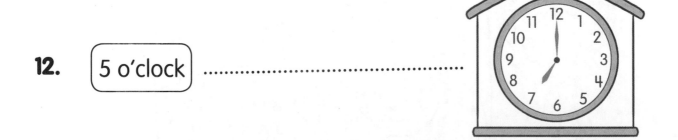

13. 11 o'clock ....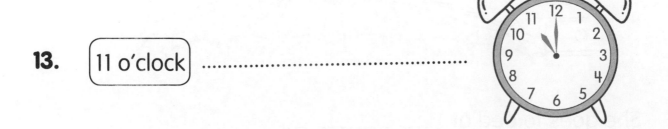

Practice 3   Telling Time to the Half Hour

Match the clock to the correct time.

1.

• half past 5

• half past 2

• half past 9

• half past 7

• half past 8

Color the clock faces that show the correct time.

2. It is half past 6. ··································

3. It is half past 10. ··································

4. It is half past 11. ··································

5. It is half past 1. ··································

6. It is half past 5. ··································

Name: _____ Date: _____

The children go to the zoo with their parents.
Look at the pictures.
Write the correct times.

7. They visit the bird and butterfly area at _____.

8. They look at the bears at _____.

The pictures show what each child does on a Sunday.
Look at the pictures.
Then fill in the blanks.

Example

Jamal rides the bike with
his Dad at ___half past 9___.

9. At _____, Ashley
enjoys lunch with her
mother.

10. Pedro goes to the bowling alley with his Grandpa at

_____.

11. John walks his dog at

_____.

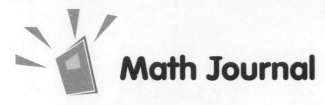 **Math Journal**

Look at each clock.
Then write about an activity you do at that time.
Use **o'clock** or **half past** in your sentences.

What I do in the morning...

_____

_____

What I do in the afternoon...

_____

_____

What I do at night ...

_____

_____

Put On Your Thinking Cap!

Challenging Practice

Use the calendar to find the answer.

September						
Sun.	Mon.	Tue.	Wed.	Thu.	Fri.	Sat.
		1	2	3	4	5
6	7	8	9	10	11	12
13	14	15	16	17	18	19
20	21	22	23	24	25	26
27	28	29	30			

1. What is the date of the second Monday? _____

2. How many Wednesdays are there? _____

3. What is the date of the third Thursday? _____

4. What day of the week is September 25? _____

5. a. Which day of the week will the next month begin on?
   _____

   b. What will be the date? _____

6. a. Which day of the week did the last month end on?
   _____

   b. What was the date?

Put On Your Thinking Cap!

Problem Solving

Aunt Betsy is baking some muffins for Lori.
Look at the pictures.
Write 1, 2, 3, and 4 to show the correct order.

_____

_____

_____

_____

Chapter Review/Test

Vocabulary

Choose the correct word.

week	days
months	year
calendar	

1. There are 7 _____ in one _____.

2. There are 12 _____ in one _____.

3. The _____ orders time into days, weeks, and months.

Concepts and Skills

Match.

4. October •   • is the season that comes before winter.

5. February •   • comes before Saturday.

6. Sunday •   • is the tenth month of the year.

7. Friday •   • is the first day of the week.

8. Fall •   • is the only month with 28 or 29 days.

9. Write the time.

_____   _____   _____

Fill in the blanks.

10. School starts at _____.

11. School is over at _____.

12. Name your favorite season. Explain your answer.

    _____.

    _____

Problem Solving
Solve.

13. Today is May 12, 2010.
    What will the date be in one week?

14. Leon's birthday is on March 15.
    Angelina's is one week after Leon's.
    When is Angelina's birthday?

Cumulative Review

for Chapters 14 and 15

Concepts and Skills

Add.
Use doubles facts or doubles plus one facts.

1. 6 + 6 = _____

2. 8 + 7 = _____

Add mentally.

3. 12 + 5 = _____

4. 24 + 3 = _____

5. 21 + 8 = _____

6. 32 + 4 = _____

Add mentally.

7. 10 + 23 = _____

8. 18 + 10 = _____

Subtract mentally.

9. 11 – 5 = _____

10. 18 – 9 = _____

11. 23 – 2 = _____

12. 27 – 2 = _____

Subtract mentally.

13. $26 - 10 =$ _____

14. $35 - 10 =$ _____

15. $30 - 20 =$ _____

16. $27 - 20 =$ _____

Fill in the blanks.

17. There are _____ months in one year.

18. _____ is the sixth month of the year.

19. _____ is the month that comes before December.

20. _____ months have 31 days.

21. The four seasons are spring, _____,
_____, and _____.

© Marshall Cavendish International (Singapore) Private Limited.

Match.

22.

•   • half past 10

23.

•   • 7 o'clock

24.

•   • 6 o'clock

25.

•   • half past 2

Ethan does some activities on a Sunday.
Write the time for each activity.

26.  Ethan eats his breakfast

at _____.

27.  Ethan swims at _____.

28.  Ethan reads his book at

_____.

Which clock shows the correct time?
Put a ✓ in the ⬚.

29.

10 o'clock ⬚

30.

half past 4 ⬚

Problem Solving

SEPTEMBER						
Sunday	Monday	Tuesday	Wednesday	Thursday	Friday	Saturday
		1	2	3	4	5
6	7	8	9	10	11	12
13	14	15	16	17	18	19
20	21	22	23	24	25	26
27	28	29	30			

Fill in the blanks.
Use the calendar to help you.

31.   The third day of the month falls on a _____.

32.   There are _____ days in this month.

33.   The date of the third Thursday of the month is

_____.

34.   The day of the week after September 15 is _____.

35.   The first day of September is on a _____.

So, the last day of August was on a _____.

Use the calendar on pg 133.

SEPTEMBER						
Sunday	Monday	Tuesday	Wednesday	Thursday	Friday	Saturday
		1	2	3	4	5
6	7	8	9	10	11	12
13	14	15	16	17	18	19
20	21	22	23	24	25	26
27	28	29	30			

36. Fill in the blanks with the dates for all the Fridays.

_____, _____, _____, _____

Fill in the blanks. Use your answers in Exercise 36 to help you.

37. The date for each Friday is _____ more than the date for the Friday before.

38. This is because there are _____ days in a week.

Problem Solving

Solve.
Show your work.

39. Laila ice skates for three weeks.
She ice skates only from Monday to Thursday for each week.
How many days does she ice skate in all?

She ice skates for _____ days.

CHAPTER 16 Numbers to 100

Practice 1   Counting to 100

Count in tens and ones.
Fill in the blanks.

Example

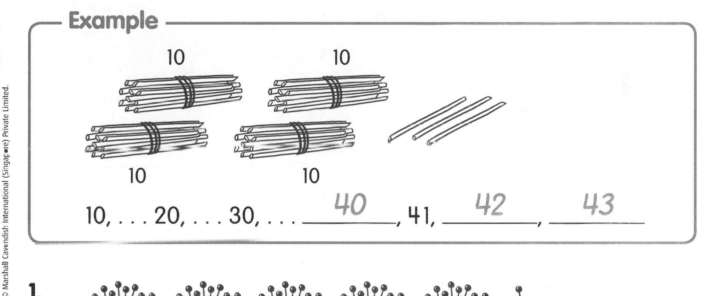

10, . . . 20, . . . 30, . . . _____40____, 41, ___42___, ___43___

1.

10, . . . 20, . . . 30, . . . 40, . . . _____, _____, _____

2.

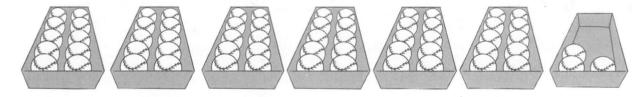

10, . . . 20, . . . 30, . . . 40, . . . 50, . . . 60, _____,

_____, _____

3.

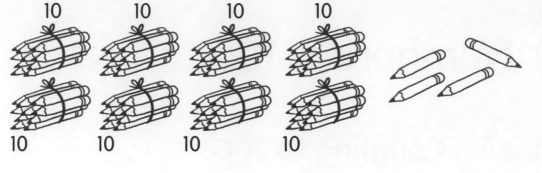

_____, . . . 20, . . . 30, . . . 40, . . . 50, . . . 60, . . . 70, . . .

_____, _____, 82, 83, _____

Write the number.

4. forty-nine   _____

5. sixty-eight   _____

6. ninety-five   _____

7. eighty-seven   _____

8. fifty-six   _____

9. seventy-three   _____

10. ninety-two   _____

Match the number to the words.

11. 40 ●   ● fifty-one

     51 ●   ● seventy-two

     72 ●   ● forty

     88 ●   ● eighty-eight

     56 ●   ● sixty-five

     65 ●   ● fifty-six

     90 ●   ● thirty-three

     33 ●   ● ninety

Find the missing numbers.

12. 60 and 4 make _____.

13. 5 and 70 make _____.

14. 50 and _____ make 53.

15. _____ and 4 make 84.

16. 40 + 5 = _____

17. _____ + 80 = 88

Circle a group of 10.
Estimate how many there are.
Then count.

18.

Estimate: _____   Count: _____

19.

Estimate: _____   Count: _____

Practice 2 Place Value

Look at the pictures.
Then fill in the blanks.

Example

-10- -10- -10- -10-

_____45_____ = _____4_____ tens _____5_____ ones

1.

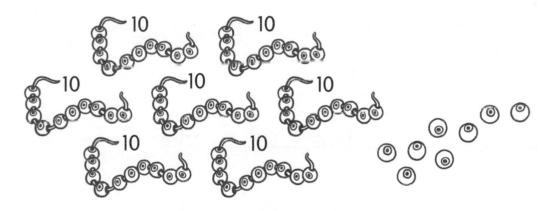

_____ = _____ tens _____ ones

2.

_____ = _____ tens _____ ones

3.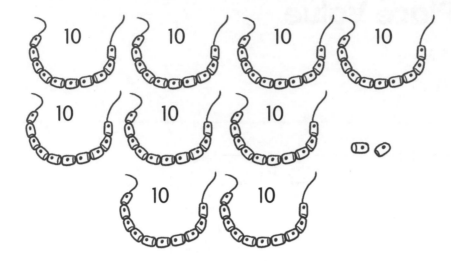

_____ = _____ tens _____ ones

4.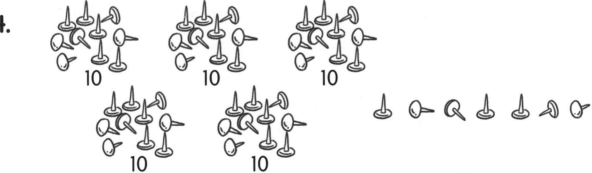

_____ = _____ tens _____ ones

5.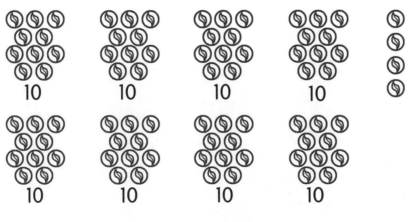

_____ = _____ tens _____ ones

Count the base-ten blocks.
Then fill in the blanks.

Example

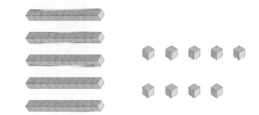

___69___ = ___6___ tens ___9___ ones

___60___ + ___9___ = ___69___

6.

_____ = _____ tens _____ ones

_____ + _____ = _____

7.

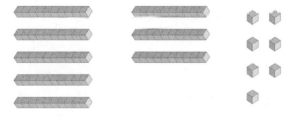

_____ = _____ tens _____ ones

_____ + _____ = _____

Fill in the place-value charts.

8.

Tens	Ones

9.

Tens	Ones

10.

Tens	Ones

11.

Tens	Ones

12.

Tens	Ones

Practice 3   Comparing, Ordering, and Patterns

Find the missing numbers.

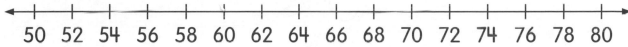

50 52 54 56 58 60 62 64 66 68 70 72 74 76 78 80

Example

2 more than 50 is ___52___.

2 less than 66 is ___64___.

1. 2 more than 54 is _____.   2. _____ is 2 more than 66.

3. 2 less than 78 is _____.   4. _____ is 2 less than 74.

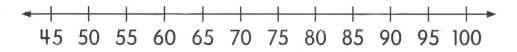

45 50 55 60 65 70 75 80 85 90 95 100

5. 5 more than 50 is _____.   6. 10 more than 85 is _____.

7. 5 less than 65 is _____.   8. _____ is 10 less than 100.

9. _____ is 5 more than 75.   10. _____ is 5 less than 75.

Circle the greater number.

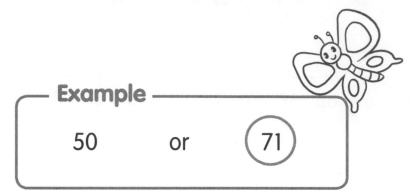

Example

50　　or　　⟨71⟩

11.　72　　or　　87　　　**12.**　92　　or　　69

13.　54　　or　　45　　　**14.**　67　　or　　76

15.　86　　or　　83　　　**16.**　94　　or　　98

Color the number that is less.

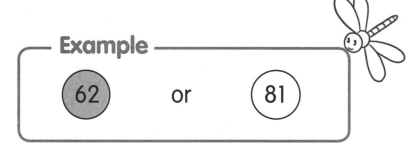

Example

(62)　　or　　(81)

17. (59)　or　△71△　　**18.** (68)　or　△93△

19. (79)　or　□97□　　**20.** □84□　or　(48)

21. (62)　or　(67)　　**22.** (96)　or　(91)

Name: _____   Date: _____

Compare the numbers.
Then fill in the blanks.

23.

The least number is _____.

The greatest number is _____.

24.

The least number is _____.

The greatest number is _____.

25. Order the numbers from greatest to least.

_____, _____, _____, _____
greatest   least

Use the numbers to fill in the blanks.

26. The greatest number is _____.

27. The least number is _____.

28. _____, _____, and _____ are less than 84.

29. _____ and _____ are greater than 84.

30. 67 is greater than _____ but less than 100.

31. 92 is less than _____ but greater than 84.

Complete each number pattern.

32. 50, 51, 52, _____, 54, 55, _____, _____, 58

33. 73, 72, 71, _____, _____, 68, _____

34. _____, 87, 89, _____, 93, _____

35. 99, _____, 95, 93, _____, _____

36. 50, 60, _____, 80, _____, _____

37. 93, 83, 73, _____, _____, 43, _____

Put on Your Thinking Cap!

Challenging Practice

Read each clue.
Cross out the numbers that are incorrect.
Fill in the blanks.

1.

The mystery number is less than 90.
It is greater 56.
The mystery number is _____.

2.

The mystery number is greater than 50 but less than 70.
It is 5 more than 60.
The mystery number is _____.

3.

The mystery number is less than 90 but greater than 63.
It is 1 less than 80.
The mystery number is _____.

Put on Your Thinking Cap!

Problem Solving

Use the chart to complete the following number patterns.
Explain the rule for the number pattern.

1	2	3	4	5	6	7	8	9	10
11	12	13	14	15	16	17	18	19	20
21	22	23	24	25	26	27	28	29	30
31	32	33	34	35	36	37	38	39	40
41	42	43	44	45	46	47	48	49	50
51	52	53	54	55	56	57	58	59	60
61	62	63	64	65	66	67	68	69	70
71	72	73	74	75	76	77	78	79	80
81	82	83	84	85	86	87	88	89	90
91	92	93	94	95	96	97	98	99	100

Example

22, 25, 28, 31, __34__, __37__, __40__

Rule: _Counting on in steps of 3 from the_
number before it

Or _Adding 3 to the number before it_

1. 41, 46, 51, 56, _____, _____, _____

Rule: _____

2. 30, 36, 42, 48, _____, _____, _____

Rule: _____

3. 10, 20, 30, 40, _____, _____, _____

Rule: _____

4. 81, 78, 75, 72, _____, _____, _____

Rule: _____

5. 90, 85, 80, 75, _____, _____, _____

Rule: _____

6. 80, 70, 60, 50, _____, _____, _____

Rule: _____

© Marshall Cavendish International (Singapore) Private Limited.

Chapter Review/Test

Vocabulary

Choose the correct word.

| compare | estimate | number line |

1. You _____ numbers by finding which number is greater than or less than the other.

2. When you do not need an exact number, you can _____.

3. A _____ is used to compare numbers.

Concepts and Skills

Fill in the blanks.

4. Write ninety-eight as a number. _____

5. Write 74 in word form. _____

6. 80 and 7 make _____.

7. 64 = _____ tens _____ ones

8. _____ is 6 more than 54.

Compare.

9. Circle the greatest number.

10. Circle the least number.

Estimate then count.

11. Estimate the number of bowling pins.
Then count the exact number.

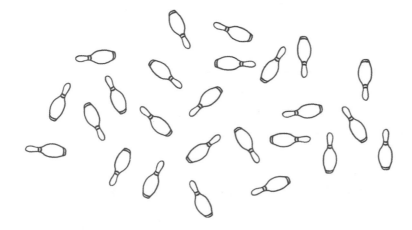

Estimate: _____

Count: _____

CHAPTER 17 Addition and Subtraction to 100

Practice 1 Addition Without Regrouping

Add by counting on.

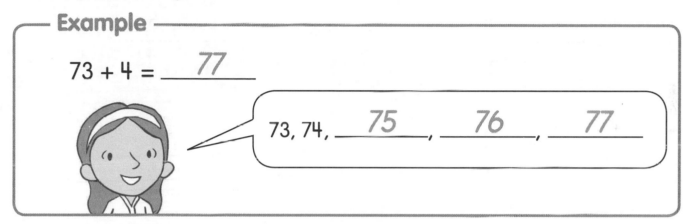

Example

73 + 4 = ___77___

73, 74, ___75___, ___76___, ___77___

1. 85 + 3 = _____

85, _____, _____, _____

2. 62 + 6 = _____

62, _____, _____, _____,

_____, _____, _____

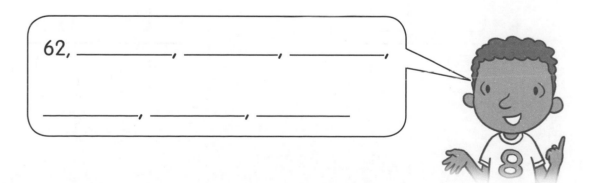

Add.

3.

```
    5   3
+       4
_____
```

4.

```
    9   2
+       7
_____
```

5.

```
    8   3
+       5
_____
```

6.

```
    4   4
+       5
_____
```

7.

```
        2
+   6   3
_____
```

8.

```
        4
+   7   3
_____
```

Fill in the missing numbers.

9. 5 + 82 = _____

```
  ☐ ☐
+ ☐ ☐
_____
  ☐ ☐
```

10. 93 + 2 = _____

```
  ☐ ☐
+ ☐ ☐
_____
  ☐ ☐
```

Add.

11.
```
    2   0
+   5   0
─────────
```

12.
```
    6   0
+   2   3
─────────
```

13.
```
    3   7
+   4   0
─────────
```

14.
```
    5   3
+   4   5
─────────
```

15.
```
    6   3
+   2   4
─────────
```

16.
```
    4   7
+   1   2
─────────
```

Fill in the missing numbers.

17. 56 + 23 = _____

```
      ☐   ☐
+     ☐   ☐
─────────────
      ☐   ☐
```

18. 86 + 13 = _____

```
      ☐   ☐
+     ☐   ☐
─────────────
      ☐   ☐
```

Match.

19.

 •

 •

$\boxed{77}$ •

$\triangle\!42$ •

$\bigcirc\!90$ •

• 20 + 70

• 0 + 42

• 72 + 5

• 54 + 31

• 40 + 49

Practice 2   Addition with Regrouping

Add.

1.
$$\begin{array}{r} 4\ 8 \\ +\quad 5 \\ \hline \end{array}$$

2.
$$\begin{array}{r} 5\ 7 \\ +\quad 8 \\ \hline \end{array}$$

3.
$$\begin{array}{r} 7 \\ +\ 6\ 4 \\ \hline \end{array}$$

4.
$$\begin{array}{r} 5\ 9 \\ +\quad 4 \\ \hline \end{array}$$

5.
$$\begin{array}{r} 7\ 3 \\ +\quad 9 \\ \hline \end{array}$$

6.
$$\begin{array}{r} 5 \\ +\ 8\ 6 \\ \hline \end{array}$$

Fill in the missing numbers.

7. $4 + 66 =$ _____

8. $89 + 8 =$ _____

9. Matt drops a ball into the number machine below.
What happens to the number on the ball?

Write the number in the 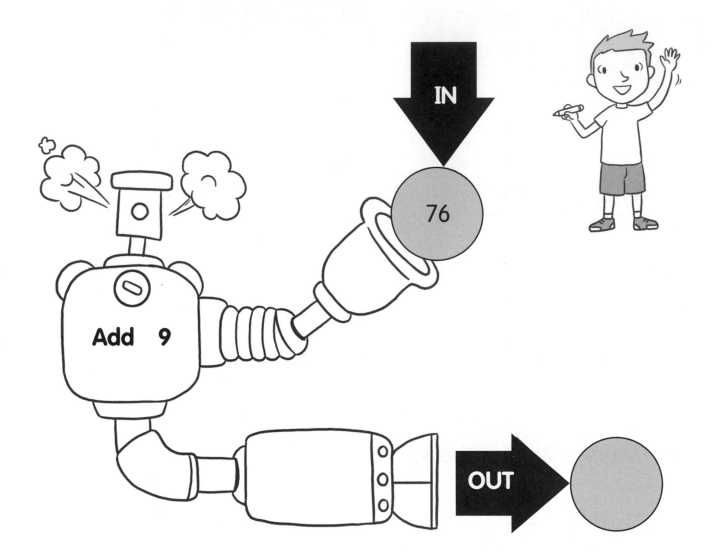.

IN

76

Add 9

OUT

Add.

10.
```
    2   7
+   2   8
_____
```

11.
```
    8   6
+   1   4
_____
```

12.
```
    2   5
+   3   7
_____
```

13.
```
    4   4
+   3   7
_____
```

14.
```
    3   9
+   2   1
_____
```

15.
```
    3   6
+   5   4
_____
```

Fill in the missing numbers.

16.   19 + 14 = _____

```
    ☐  ☐
+   ☐  ☐
_____
    ☐  ☐
```

17.   58 + 36 = _____

```
    ☐  ☐
+   ☐  ☐
_____
    ☐  ☐
```

Add.
Then answer the question.

18. $52 + 19 =$ _____ (Y)

19. $58 + 6 =$ _____ (B)

20. $67 + 18 =$ _____ (A)

21. $48 + 38 =$ _____ (E)

22. $7 + 59 =$ _____ (D)

23. $43 + 57 =$ _____ (R)

24. $39 + 49 =$ _____ (T)

25. $27 + 49 =$ _____ (D)

26. $56 + 35 =$ _____ (E)

What toy is named after President Theodore Roosevelt?

Match the letters to the answers below to find out.

☐	☐	☐	☐	☐		☐	☐	☐	☐
88	86	66	76	71		64	91	85	100

27. Ron drops a ball into a number machine.
Which ball is it?

Write the number in the ◯.

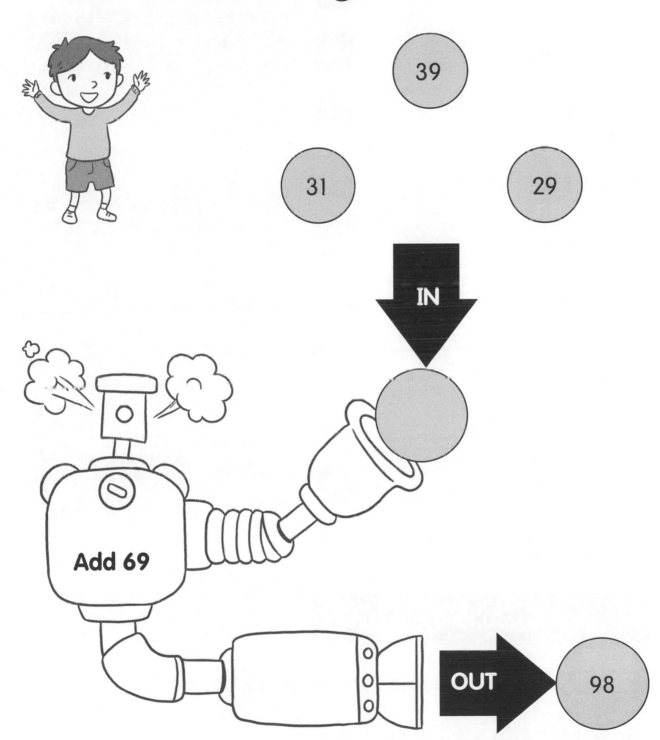

39

31

29

IN

Add 69

OUT → 98

Add.
Then solve the riddle.

28. 45 + 7 = ___*52*___

29. 52 + 5 = _____

30. 2 + 78 = _____

31. 72 + 8 = _____

32. 2 + 70 = _____

33. 64 + 19 = _____

34. 28 + 40 = _____

35. 40 + 30 = _____

36. 61 + 16 = _____

37. 17 + 63 = _____

T
A
S
N
R
I
H
D
F
S

Which fish do you find in space?

Match the letters to the answers below to find out.

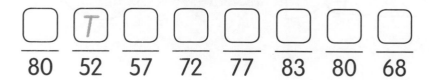

___	*T*	___	___	___	___	___	___
80	52	57	72	77	83	80	68

Practice 3 Subtraction Without Regrouping

Count back to subtract.

Example

$67 - 4 =$ ___63___

67, 66, __65__, __64__, __63__

1. $95 - 3 =$ _____

95, 94, _____, _____

2. $88 - 5 =$ _____

88, 87, _____, _____,

_____, _____

3. $79 - 6 =$ _____

79, 78, _____, _____,

_____, _____, _____

Subtract.

4.
$$\begin{array}{r} 5 \ 8 \\ - \quad\ 3 \\ \hline \end{array}$$

5.
$$\begin{array}{r} 6 \ 9 \\ - \quad\ 4 \\ \hline \end{array}$$

6.
$$\begin{array}{r} 7 \ 4 \\ - \quad\ 3 \\ \hline \end{array}$$

7.
$$\begin{array}{r} 6 \ 7 \\ - \quad\ 5 \\ \hline \end{array}$$

8.
$$\begin{array}{r} 9 \ 6 \\ - \quad\ 3 \\ \hline \end{array}$$

9.
$$\begin{array}{r} 8 \ 8 \\ - \quad\ 7 \\ \hline \end{array}$$

Fill in the missing numbers.

10. $79 - 6 =$ _____

$$\begin{array}{r} \square \ \square \\ - \ \square \ \square \\ \hline \square \ \square \end{array}$$

11. $99 - 5 =$ _____

$$\begin{array}{r} \square \ \square \\ - \ \square \ \square \\ \hline \square \ \square \end{array}$$

Subtract.

12.
```
    9   5
-   2   0
_____
```

13.
```
    4   9
-   3   0
_____
```

14.
```
    7   0
-   2   0
_____
```

15.
```
    4   0
-   2   0
_____
```

16.
```
    6   8
-   3   2
_____
```

17.
```
    9   7
-   5   4
_____
```

Fill in the missing numbers.

18.   56 − 23 = _____

```
    ▢   ▢
-   ▢   ▢
_____
    ▢   ▢
```

19.   86 − 42 = _____

```
    ▢   ▢
-   ▢   ▢
_____
    ▢   ▢
```

Match.

20.

 48 •   •  83 – 10

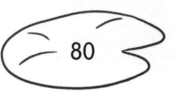 52 •   •  77 – 21

 80 •   •  90 – 10

 56 •   •  84 – 32

 60 •   •  94 – 34

73 •   •  68 – 20

Name: _____ Date: _____

Practice 4   Subtraction with Regrouping
Subtract.

1.
```
    6   4
-       8
_____
```

2.
```
    9   3
-       5
_____
```

3.
```
    7   8
-       9
_____
```

4.
```
    8   7
-       8
_____
```

5.
```
    5   0
-       2
_____
```

6.
```
    8   0
-       6
_____
```

Fill in the missing numbers.

7.   72 – 9 = _____

```
   □   □
-  □   □
_____
   □   □
```

8.   91 – 4 = _____

```
   □   □
-  □   □
_____
   □   □
```

9. Kayla drops a ball into a number machine.
Which ball is it?

Write the number in the ◯.

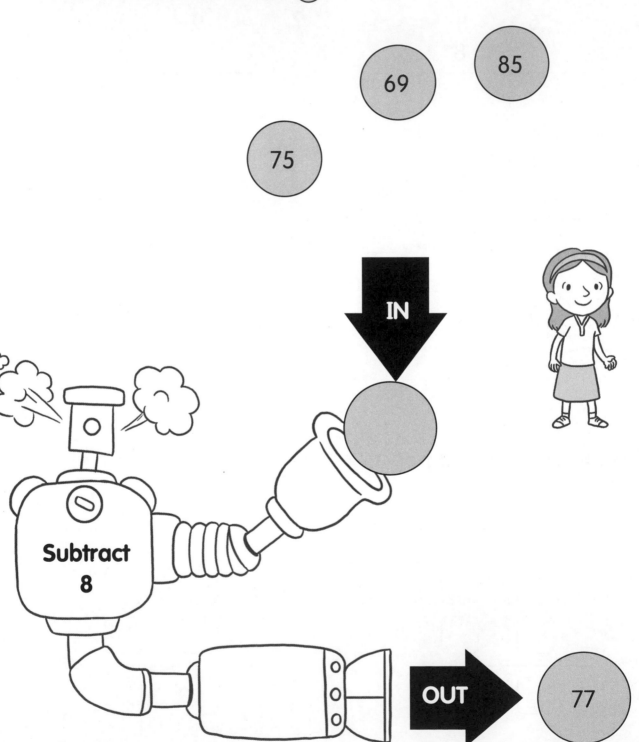

69 85

75

IN

Subtract
8

OUT 77

Subtract.

10.
```
    5   2
-   3   8
_____
```

11.
```
    7   6
-   4   9
_____
```

12.
```
    8   5
-   3   8
_____
```

13.
```
    5   3
-   4   7
_____
```

14.
```
    9   0
-   5   6
_____
```

15.
```
    7   3
-   5   6
_____
```

Fill in the missing numbers.

16.   83 – 26 = _____

17.   95 – 38 = _____

18. Ken drops a ball into a number machine.
Which ball is it?

Write the number in the ◯**.**

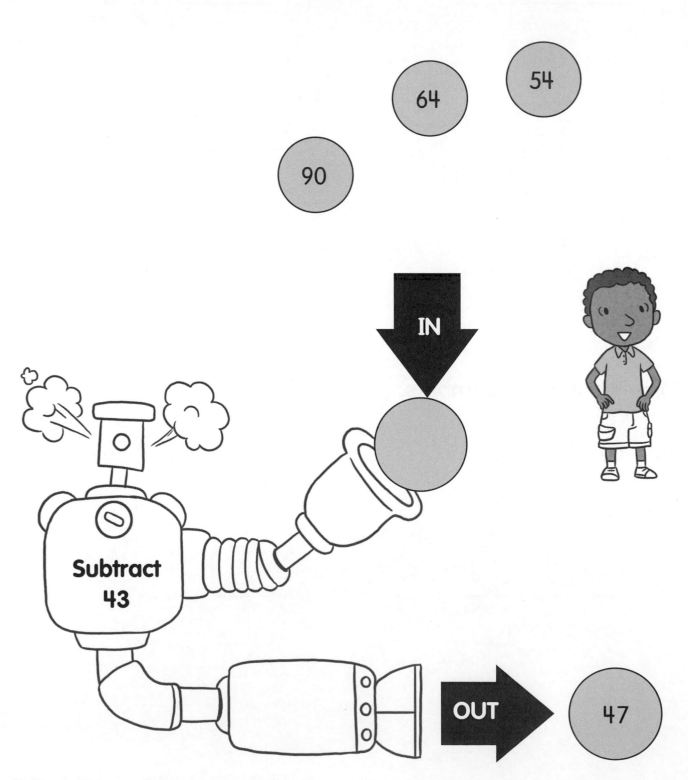

Color the correct answer.

19.

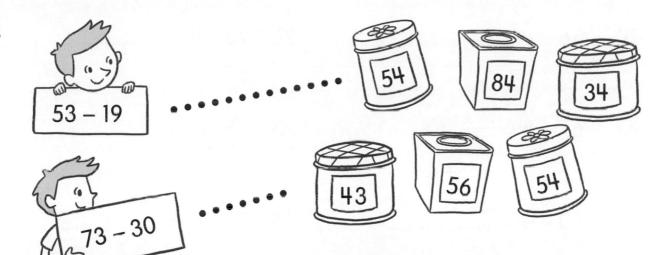

53 – 19 54   84   34

73 – 30 43   56   54

81 – 46 34   35   45

60 – 27 43   33   47

70 – 30 40   63   33

90 – 5 85   53   67

Subtract.

20. $56 - 8 =$ _____

21. $73 - 4 =$ _____

22. $67 - 8 =$ _____

23. $75 - 9 =$ _____

24. $50 - 40 =$ _____

25. $87 - 11 =$ _____

26. $90 - 50 =$ _____

27. $93 - 20 =$ _____

28. $58 - 18 =$ _____

29. $61 - 14 =$ _____

30. $47 - 39 =$ _____

31. $53 - 27 =$ _____

32. $30 - 28 =$ _____

33. $90 - 88 =$ _____

 # Put on Your Thinking Cap!

Challenging Practice

The Hundred Train is here!
On its cars are two numbers that add to 100.

Example

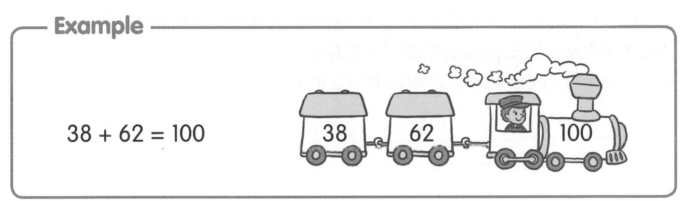

$38 + 62 = 100$

There are many pairs of numbers that make 100.
Write a pair of numbers on each train.

1.

2.

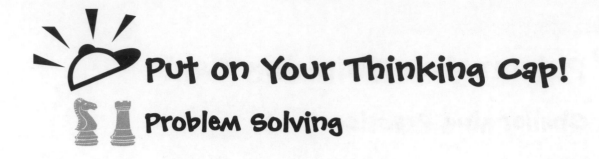

Put on Your Thinking Cap!

Problem Solving

Rosa buys stickers each day.

She buys 1 sticker on the 1st day, 2 stickers on the 2nd day,

3 stickers on the 3rd day and 4 stickers on the 4th day.

Rosa follows this pattern for 10 days.

How many stickers does she have in all?

Chapter Review/Test

Concepts and Skills

Add.

1.

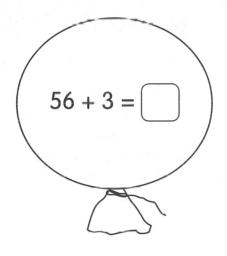

$56 + 3 = \boxed{}$

2.

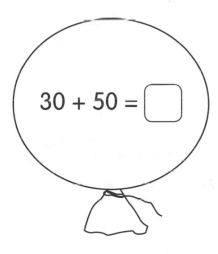

$30 + 50 = \boxed{}$

3.

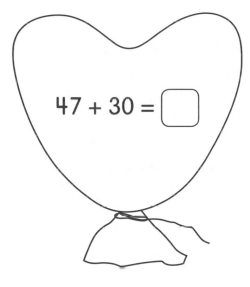

$47 + 30 = \boxed{}$

4.

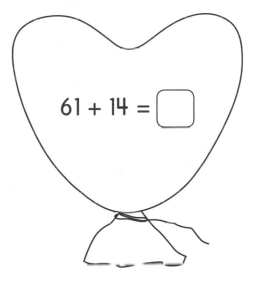

$61 + 14 = \boxed{}$

5.

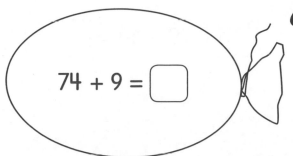

$74 + 9 = \boxed{}$

6.

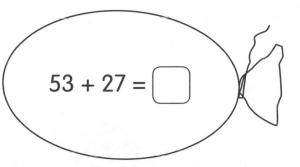

$53 + 27 = \boxed{}$

Subtract.

7.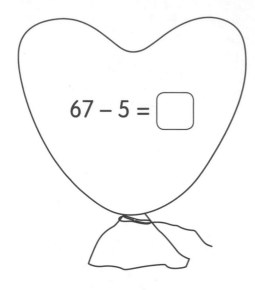

$$67 - 5 = \boxed{}$$

8.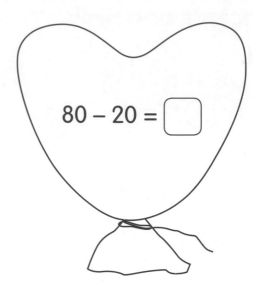

$$80 - 20 = \boxed{}$$

9.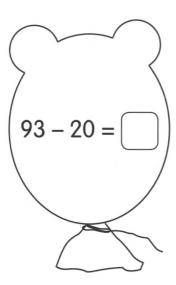

$$93 - 20 = \boxed{}$$

10.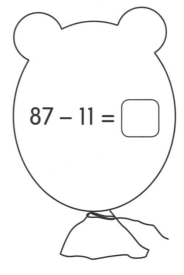

$$87 - 11 = \boxed{}$$

11.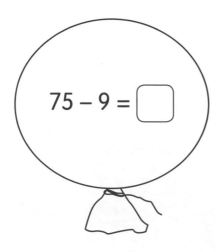

$$75 - 9 = \boxed{}$$

12.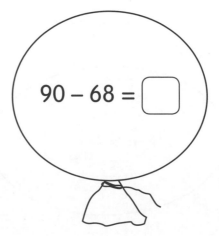

$$90 - 68 = \boxed{}$$

Cumulative Review

for Chapters 16 and 17

Concepts and Skills

Count in tens and ones.
Fill in the blanks.

1. _____, ...20, ...30, ...40, ..._____, ..._____,

..._____, ...80, _____, _____, _____, _____.

Write the number in words.

2. 57 _____

3. 93 _____

Write the number.

4. forty-eight _____

5. sixty-nine _____

Fill in the blanks.

6. 4 and 90 make _____.

7. _____ and 5 make 75.

Estimate.
Then count.

8.

Estimate _____

Count _____

Fill in the blanks.

9. _____ = _____ tens _____ ones

Name: _____   Date: _____

Count the base-ten blocks.
Fill in the blanks.

10.

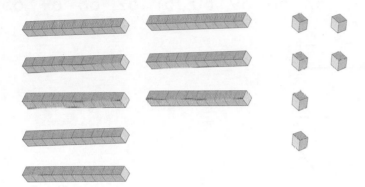

_____ = _____ tens _____ ones

_____ + _____ = _____

Fill in the place-value charts.

11.

Tens	Ones

12.

Tens	Ones

Find the missing numbers.

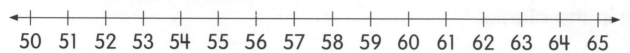

13. 2 more than 54 is _____.

14. 3 less than 65 is _____.

15. _____ is 2 more than 55.

16. _____ is 2 less than 63.

17.

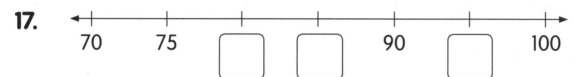

Compare.
Fill in the blanks.

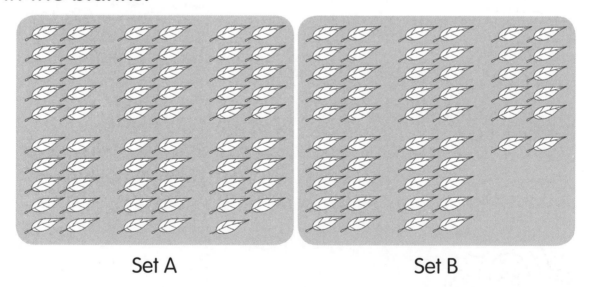

Set A   Set B

18. Set _____ is _____ more than Set _____.

19. Set _____ has more.

Name: _____ **Date:** _____

Color the greater number.

20. (71) or (80)   **21.** (45) or (54)

Color the number that is less.

22. /35\ or /51\   **23.** /91\ or /89\

Fill in the blanks.

24.

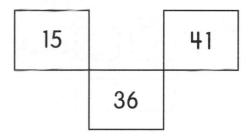

The least number is _____.

The greatest number is _____.

Order the numbers from least to greatest.

25. ⬡76 ⬡50 ⬡67

_____, _____, _____

least

Complete each number pattern.

26. 73, 72, 71, _____, _____, 68, _____

27. 50, 60, _____, 80, _____, _____

Add by counting on.

28. 82 + 7 = _____   **29.** 50 + 40 = _____

Add.

30.
$$\begin{array}{cc} 7 & 6 \\ + & 7 \\ \hline \Box & \Box \end{array}$$

31.
$$\begin{array}{cc} 2 & 6 \\ + 3 & 8 \\ \hline \Box & \Box \end{array}$$

Fill in the missing numbers.

32. 8 + 33 = _____

$$\begin{array}{cc} \Box & \Box \\ + \Box & \Box \\ \hline \Box & \Box \end{array}$$

33. 64 + 19 = _____

$$\begin{array}{cc} \Box & \Box \\ + \Box & \Box \\ \hline \Box & \Box \end{array}$$

Count back to subtract.

34. 97 – 6 = _____

35. 50 – 30 = _____

Subtract.

36.
$$\begin{array}{cc} 6 & 3 \\ - & 7 \\ \hline \Box & \Box \end{array}$$

37.
$$\begin{array}{cc} 9 & 0 \\ - & 6 \\ \hline \Box & \Box \end{array}$$

Fill in the missing numbers.

38. 45 – 6 = _____

$$\begin{array}{cc} \Box & \Box \\ - \Box & \Box \\ \hline \Box & \Box \end{array}$$

39. 73 – 58 = _____

$$\begin{array}{cc} \Box & \Box \\ - \Box & \Box \\ \hline \Box & \Box \end{array}$$

Problem Solving

Solve.

40. A number is less than 30 but greater than 10.
It has 6 in the ones place.
What are the possible numbers?

41. A number is 65 when you subtract 6 then add 7.
What is the number?
Circle the number.

58   64   71   52

42. Write an addition sentence to make 100.
One of the numbers must have 3 in the ones place.

_____ + _____ = 100

There is more than one correct answer.

Fill in the blank.
Choose a number in the box.

43.

63   40   36   88

62 – _____ = 26

CHAPTER 18 Multiplication and Division

Practice 1 Adding the Same Number

Count the number of groups.
Then count the number of bugs in each group.
Write the numbers in the blanks.

Example

We are in 2 groups.

There are 3 of us in each group.

3 + 3 = ___6___ •••••••••••••• 2 threes = ___6___

1.

2 + 2 + 2 + 2 + 2 = _____ •••••••• 5 twos = _____

Count the number of groups.
Then count the number of bugs in each group.
Write the numbers in the blanks.

2.

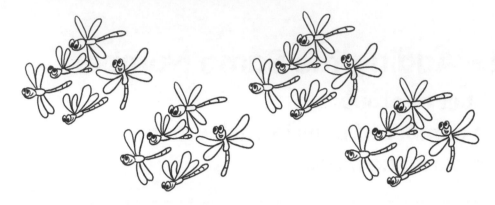

5 + 5 + 5 + 5 = _____ . . . . .4 fives = _____

3.

4 + 4 + 4 = _____ . . . . .3 fours = _____

4.

8 + 8 = _____ . . . . .2 eights = _____

Name: _____   **Date:** _____

Look at the pictures.
Then fill in the blanks.

5.

_____ + _____ + _____ + _____ + _____ + _____

= _____

_____ twos = _____

There are _____ snails in all.

6.

_____ + _____ + _____ + _____ = _____

_____ fours = _____

There are _____ shrimps in all.

**Look at the pictures.
Then fill in the blanks.**

Example

There are _____10_____ lobsters.　　2 __*fives*__ = 10

7.

There are _____ crabs.　　　4 _____ = _____

8.

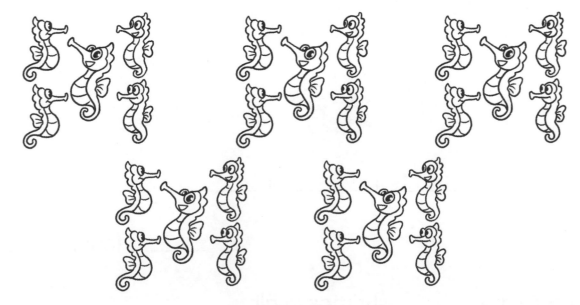

There are _____ seahorses.　　5 _____ = _____

Look at the picture.
Then fill in the blanks.

9.   A starfish has _____ arms.

6 _*fives*_ = _____

6 starfishes have _____ arms.

10.   Each dress has 5 buttons.

3 _____ = _____

3 dresses have _____ buttons.

11.   One flower has _____ petals.

6 _____ = _____

6 flowers have _____ petals.

Look at the picture.
Then fill in the blanks.

12.   Each plant has _____ leaves.

5 _____ = _____

5 plants have _____ leaves.

13.   An octopus has _____ arms.

4 _____ = _____

4 octopuses have _____ arms.

Practice 2 Sharing Equally

Look at the pack of fish crackers.
Then fill in the blanks.

1.

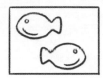 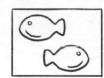 

There are _____ fish crackers in all.

How many fish crackers are in each pack? _____

2.

There are _____ fish crackers in all.

How many fish crackers are in each pack? _____

Look at the pictures.
Then fill in the blanks.

3.

There are _____ mice in all.

There are _____ tubs.

There are _____ mice in each tub.

4.

There are _____ monkeys in all.

There are _____ trees.

There are _____ monkeys on each tree.

Name: _____ Date: _____

Look at the pictures.
Then fill in the blanks.

5.

There are _____ dogs in all.

There are _____ dog houses.

There is _____ dog in each dog house.

6.

There are _____ cats in all.

There are _____ baskets.

There are _____ cats in each basket.

Fill in the blanks.

Dylan is cleaning the shoe rack.
He has to put 8 shoes equally into 4 groups.

He puts 1 shoe in each group.

Then he puts 1 more in each group.

Example

Each group has _____2_____ shoes.

Name: _____ **Date:** _____

Fill in the blanks.

7. Martin is in the garden.
He has to put 10 flowers
equally into 2 groups.

Martin puts 1 flower in each group.
Help Martin put the rest of the flowers equally in each group.

Each group has _____ flowers.

8. Martin is in the library now.
He has to put 15 books
equally into 5 groups.

Martin puts 2 books in each group.
Help Martin put the rest of the books equally in each group.

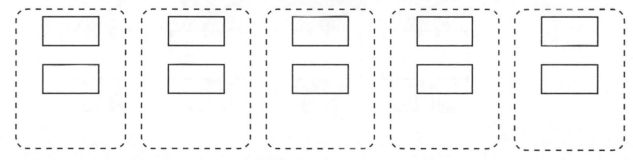

Each group has _____ books.

Draw.
Then fill in the blanks.

9.   There are 12 peanuts.
     Draw an equal number of peanuts in each bag.

     There are _____ in each bag.

10. There are 16 marbles.
     They are shared equally by 4 children.
     In each bag, draw an equal number of marbles
     for each child.

     Each child gets _____ marbles.

Fill in the blanks.

11. There are 10 toys.
Suki packs them into 5 boxes equally.
How many toys are in each box?

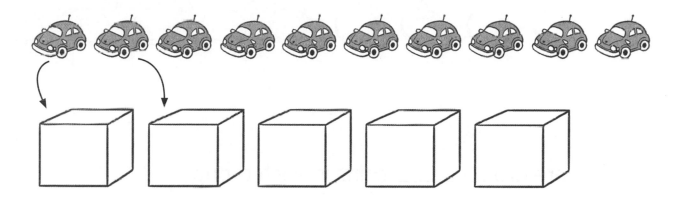

There are _____ toys in each box.

12. There are 6 balloons.
They are shared equally by 3 children.
How many balloons does each child get?

Each child gets _____ balloons.

Fill in the blanks.

13. Put 18 coins into 3 equal groups.

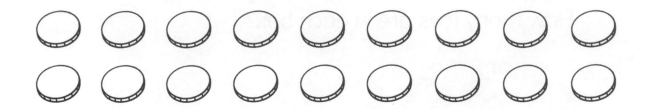

There are _____ coins in each group.

14. Put 20 pencils into 5 equal groups.

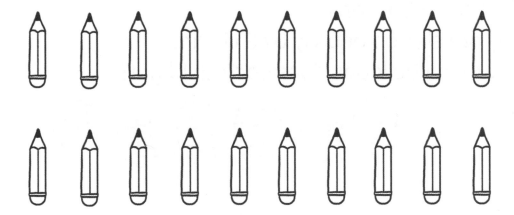

There are _____ pencils in each group.

Practice 3 Finding the Number of Groups

Circle.
Then fill in the blanks.

Example

There are 10 children.
Circle groups of 5.

There are _____2_____ groups of 5 children.

---

1. There are 16 fishes.
Circle groups of 4.

There are _____ groups of 4 fishes.

Circle.
Then fill in the blanks.

2.   There are 15 oranges.
     Circle groups of 3.

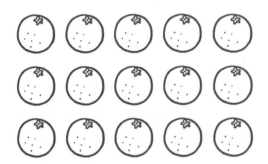

     There are _____ groups of 3 oranges.

3.   12 children go skating.
     Circle groups of 4.

     There are _____ groups of 4 children.

Circle.
Then fill in the blanks.

4.   There are 18 muffins.
     Circle the muffins in groups of 3.

     There are _____ groups of 3 muffins.

5.   There are 20 apples.
     Circle the apples in groups of _____.

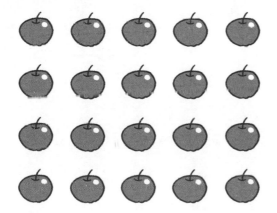

     There are _____ groups of _____ apples.

Read the story.
Then fill in the blanks.

6. There are 10 gloves.
   Pa Bear gives 2 gloves to each cub.
   How many cubs are there?

   There are _____ cubs.

7. There are 12 coins.
   Sam puts 4 coins into each coin bank.
   How many coin banks are there?

   There are _____ coin banks.

Name: _____   **Date:** _____

Read the story.
Then fill in the blanks.

8.   Josh collects stamps.
     He has 20 stamps.
     He puts 5 stamps on each page of his album.
     How many pages does he need?

     He needs _____ pages.

9.   Mrs. Lim buys 8 peaches to make jelly.
     She uses 4 peaches to make a bowl of jelly.
     How many bowls of jelly does she make?

     She makes _____ bowls of jelly.

10. Mary buys 15 oranges.
She divides them equally into a few boxes.
Each box has 5 oranges.
How many boxes does she use?

She uses _____ boxes.

11. Some squirrels share 20 nuts equally.
Each squirrel gets 2 nuts.
How many squirrels are there?

There are _____ squirrels.

 **Put On Your Thinking Cap!**

Challenging Practice

Lena collects erasers.
Look at the picture.
Then fill in the blanks.

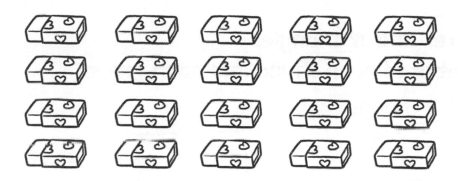

1.   Lena has _____ erasers.

2.   She puts the erasers equally into 5 boxes.
     How many erasers are in each box? _____

3.   She puts the erasers equally into 4 boxes.
     How many erasers are In each box? _____

4.   She puts 10 erasers into each box.
     How many boxes does she need? _____

5.   She puts 4 erasers into each box.
     How many boxes does she need? _____

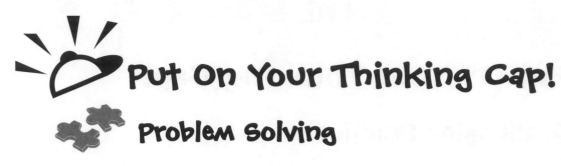

Put On Your Thinking Cap!

Problem Solving

Solve.

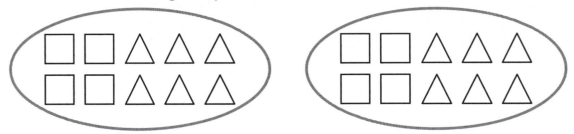

There are 8 squares and 12 triangles.

Put an equal number of each shape into each group.

1.   Put them into 2 groups.

There are _____ ☐ in each group.

There are _____ △ in each group.

There are _____ shapes in each group.

2.   Put them into 4 groups.

There are _____ ☐ in each group.

There are _____ △ in each group.

There are _____ shapes in each group.

Name: _____   Date: _____

Chapter Review/Test

Vocabulary

Choose the correct word.

same
___
groups

1.

   The picture shows equal _____.

2. By adding the _____ number, you will have 9 ⭐ in all.

Concepts and Skills

Fill in the blanks.

3.   2 + 2 + 2 = _____

       3 twos = _____

4.   5 + 5 + 5 + 5 = _____

       4 fives = _____

Match.

5.   5 threes   ●   ● 4 fours

       4 + 4 + 4 + 4   ●   ● 3 + 3 + 3 + 3 + 3

       7 + 7 + 7   ●   ● 7 threes

       3 + 3 + 3 + 3 + 3 + 3 + 3   ●   ● 3 sevens

       7 twos   ●   ● 14

6. A farmer has 16 chickens.
He puts 8 chickens in a coop.
How many coops does he need?

He needs _____ coops.

7. There are 20 seeds.
Put an equal number of seeds in each pot.

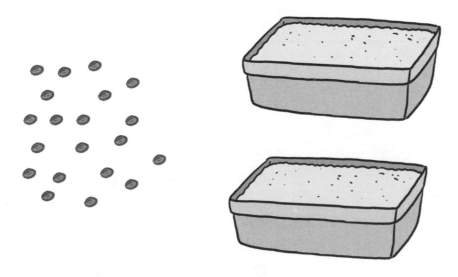

There are _____ seeds in each pot.

Name: _____   Date: _____

 Money

Practice 1 Penny, Nickel, and Dime

1. **Match.**

                    •   •   penny

                    •   •   nickel

                    •   •   dime

Write the value.

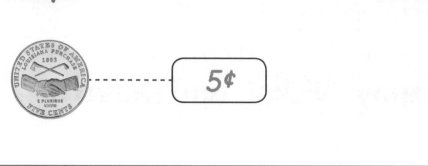

Example

5¢

2.

3.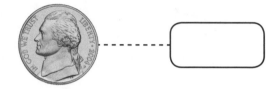

4.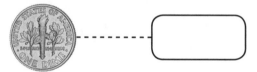

5.

Complete.

6.

Coin	Value	Name
Five cent	5¢	*nickel*
Ten cent		
One cent		

Name: _____ **Date:** _____

Keisha has these coins.

Group the pennies, nickels and dimes.
Then count on to fill in the blanks.

7. There are _____ dimes.

8. There are _____ coins in all.

9. There are _____ fewer dimes than nickels.

10. There are _____ more pennies than dimes.

Find the value.

11. pennies _____

12. nickels _____

13. dimes _____

Find the value.

Example

Skip-count by 5s.   Then count on in 1s.

__26__ ¢

Count on from the coin with the greatest value.
Count on by 10s for dimes.
Count on by 5s for nickels.
Count on by 1s for pennies.

14.

_____ ¢

15.

_____ ¢

Name: _____ Date: _____

Solve the riddle.
Circle the correct coin.

Example

You need 10 of me
to make a dime.
What am I?

16. I am silver-colored.
You need two of me to
make ten cents.
What am I?

17. Two of me has a
value of 20¢.
What am I?

Find how many of each coin are needed.
Fill in the blanks.

18.

8 ¢

_____ dimes, _____ nickels,

_____ pennies

19.

17¢

_____ dimes, _____ nickels,

_____ pennies

Find how many of each coin are needed.
Fill in the blanks.

20. _____ dimes, _____ nickels,

_____ pennies

Draw the coins to buy each thing.

Use pennies 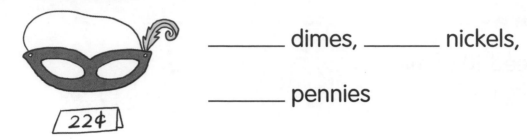 **, nickels** **5¢** **and dimes** **10¢** **.**

21. 	
22. 	
23. 	

Practice 2   Quarter

Fill in the blanks.

1.

This is a _____.

Its value is _____¢.

Complete.

2.   Exchange 1 for _____ pennies.

3.   Exchange 1  for _____ nickels.

4.   Exchange 1 for _____ pennies.

Circle the coins to show the same value.

5. 1 dime

6. 1 nickel

7. 1 quarter

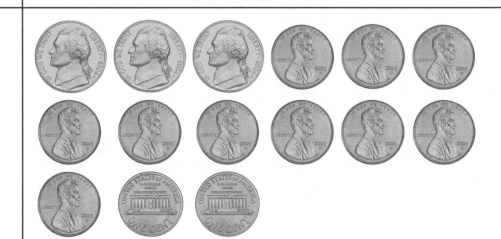

8. 1 dime

9. 1 quarter

Name: _____   Date: _____

Use pennies , nickels , dimes , and quarters .

Draw 5 ways to pay.

10.	
11.	
12.	
13.	
14.	

Draw pennies as (1¢), nickels as (5¢), dimes as (10¢), and quarters as (25¢).

Circle the coin.

Example

One   has a value of 10¢.

15. One  has a value of 25¢.

16. A   is greater than a nickel.

17. A  is less than a nickel.

18. Two nickels can be exchanged for 1  .

Fill in the blanks.

19. _____ nickels can be exchanged for 1 quarter.

20. _____ pennies can be exchanged for 1 dime.

Practice 3 Counting Money

Count on to find the value.

Example

_____36_____ ¢

1.

_____ ¢

2.

_____ ¢

3.

_____ ¢

4.

_____ ¢

5. Match.

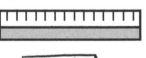

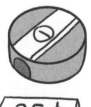

Sort the coins.

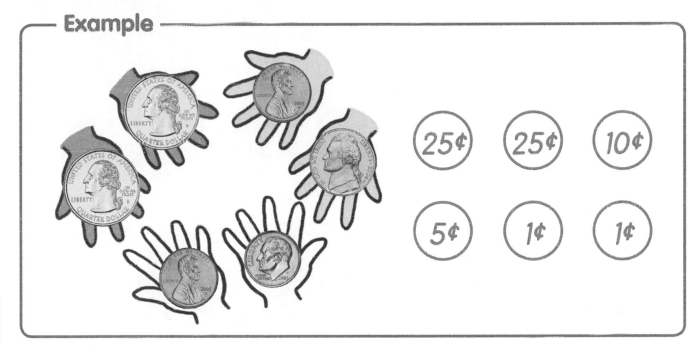

Example

6.

7.

Circle the coins you need to buy each thing.

Example

70¢

8.

80¢

9.

60¢

Name: _____   Date: _____

Circle the coins you need to buy each thing.

10.

65¢

11.

50¢

12.

19¢

Circle the coins you need to buy each thing.

13.

35¢

14.

92¢

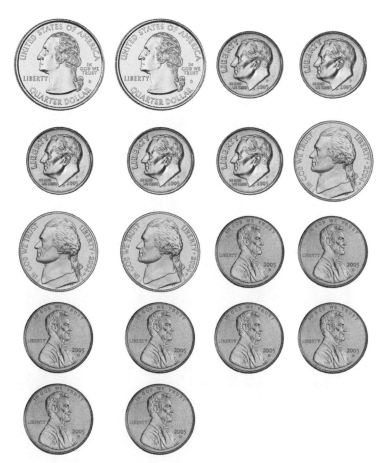

Complete the table.

Coins	Value	Draw coins to show value in another way
Example	47¢	10¢ 10¢ 10¢ 10¢ 5¢ 1¢ 1¢
15.	_____	
16.	_____	

Use pennies $\left(\text{1¢}\right)$, nickels $\left(\text{5¢}\right)$, dimes $\left(\text{10¢}\right)$, and quarters $\left(\text{25¢}\right)$.

Draw 2 ways to pay for the balloon.

87¢

17.

18.

Practice 4   Adding and Subtracting Money
Add.

1.

25¢ + 19¢ = _____¢

2.

45¢ + 15¢ = _____¢

3.

$15¢ + 15¢ = \underline{\hspace{2cm}}¢$

4.

$25¢ + 13¢ = \underline{\hspace{2cm}}¢$

Add.

┌─ **Example** ─────────────────────────────────┐

$20¢ +$

$\underline{\quad 20¢ \quad} + \underline{\quad 50¢ \quad} = \underline{\quad 70¢ \quad}$

└──┘

5. $50¢ +$

$\underline{\hspace{2cm}} + \underline{\hspace{2cm}} = \underline{\hspace{2cm}}$

6. $21¢ +$

$\underline{\hspace{2cm}} + \underline{\hspace{2cm}} = \underline{\hspace{2cm}}$

Add.

7. 8¢ +

_____ + _____ = _____

8. 17¢ +

_____ + _____ = _____

9. 13¢ +

_____ + _____ = _____

10. 6¢ +

_____ + _____ = _____

11. 38¢ +

_____ + _____ = _____

The Art Club made cards to sell.

Fill in the blanks.

Example

Neil buys ▦▦ and ⋮⋮.

___20¢___ + ___10¢___ = ___30¢___

He spends ___30¢___.

12. Zack buys  and .

_____ + _____ = _____

He spends _____.

13. Tara buys , , and .

_____ + _____ + _____ = _____

She spends _____.

14. Kerrie buys , , and .

_____ + _____ + _____ = _____

She spends _____.

15. How much do Zack and Neil spend in all?

_____ + _____ = _____

They spend _____ in all.

Subtract.

16. 55¢ – 20¢ = _____

17. 45¢ – 15¢ = _____

18. 60¢ – 5¢ = _____

19. 99¢ – 35¢ = _____

Subtract.

┌─ **Example** ──────────────────────────────────────┐
│   │
│   50¢ from 60¢   │
│   │
│   __60¢__ – __50¢__ = __10¢__   │
│   │
└──┘

20. 35¢ from 50¢

_____ – _____ = _____

21. 25¢ from 70¢

_____ – _____ = _____

22. 60¢ from 90¢

_____ – _____ = _____

23. 35¢ from 95¢

_____ – _____ = _____

Complete.

	You Have	You Buy	Your Change
Example	quarter	stamp 5¢	$25¢ - 5¢ = 20¢$
24.	quarter, dime, dime, dime	muffin 50¢	
25.	quarter, quarter	toy scooter 30¢	
26.	quarter, quarter, quarter, dime	kite 80¢	
27.	quarter, quarter	whistle 45¢	

Solve.

Example

Adam buys a pen and a doll.
How much does he spend in all?

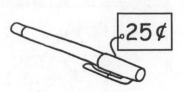

25¢ + 69¢ = 94¢

Adam spends ___94¢___ in all.

28. Sherry buys a ball.
She pays with three quarters.
How much change does she get?

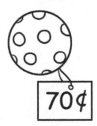

She gets _____ in change.

Solve.

29. Keri has 90¢.
She buys a paper bag.
How much does she have left?

84 ¢

She has _____ left.

30. After buying a toy bicycle, Pat has 9¢ left.
How much did he have at first?

89¢

He had _____ at first.

31. Andrew buys a pen.
Eve buys a doll.
How much less does Andrew pay than Eve?

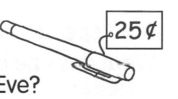

25¢

79¢

Andrew pays _____ less than Eve.

© Marshall Cavendish International (Singapore) Private Limited.

Solve.

32. Derrick has 32¢.
He wants to buy a toy bicycle.
How much more does he need?

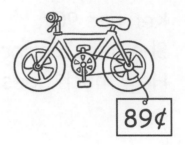

Derrick needs _____ more.

33. How much more is the pencil than the eraser?

The pencil is _____ more
than the eraser.

34. Brad spends 99¢ during break time.
What does he buy?

He buys the _____ and the _____.

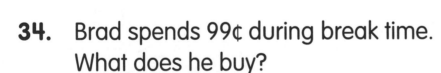

Gary and Fina are at the cafeteria.

orange
30¢

crackers
20¢

cereal
50¢

muffin
65¢

Fill in the blanks.

35. Gary buys a bowl of cereal and crackers.

How much does he spend in all? _____

36. Gary uses 50¢ to buy an orange.

How much change does he get? _____

37. Fina uses two quarters to buy an orange.

How much change does she get? _____

38. Gary buys a muffin and has 25¢ left.

How much did he have at first? _____

39. Fina has 3 dimes.
She buys her food and has 10¢ left.

What does she buy? _____

Math Journal

Susan and Marta place all their money on a table.

Write sentences about the money you see.
Say what you can buy with it.

Example

There are eight dimes.

There are _____ coins in all.

I can exchange 2 nickels with _____.

I can buy _____ with 50¢.

1. _____

2. _____

3. _____

4. _____

© Marshall Cavendish International (Singapore) Private Limited.

 Put On Your Thinking Cap!

Challenging Practice

Circle the coins to show the amount.
Use the least number of coins.

1.

50¢

2.

46¢

3.

19¢

Solve.

Does Jordan have enough money?

Example 65¢ Jordon (thought bubble: 10¢ 5¢ 10¢ 10¢)	☐ Yes. He will get change. ☑ No. He needs ___30¢___ more.
4. 70¢ (thought bubble: 25¢ 25¢ 25¢)	☐ Yes. He will get change. ☐ No. He needs _____ more.
5. 33¢ (thought bubble: 10¢ 5¢ 10¢ 10¢)	☐ Yes. He will get change. ☐ No. He needs _____ more.
6. 79¢ (thought bubble: 25¢ 5¢ 25¢)	☐ Yes. He will get change. ☐ No. He needs _____ more.

Name: _____   **Date:** _____

The picture graph shows the coins Britney has in her piggy bank.

Coins in Britney's Piggy Bank

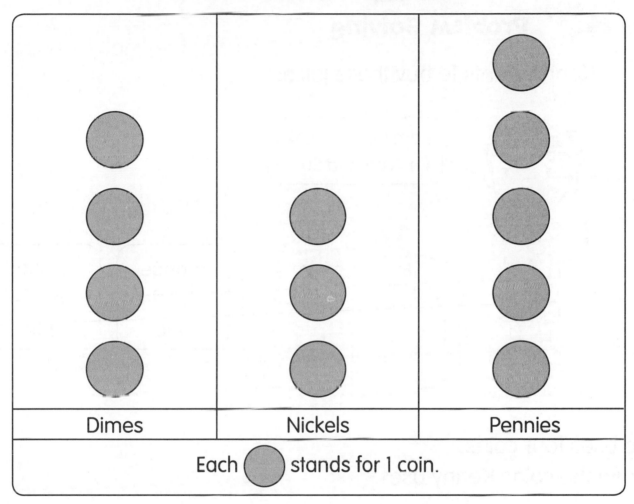

| | Dimes | Nickels | Pennies |

Each ⬤ stands for 1 coin.

Find the value of the coins in Britney's piggy bank.

_____

_____

Put On Your Thinking Cap!

Problem Solving

1. Kenny wants to buy these juices.

I am buying drinks for Alan and Sue.

Orange 30¢

Apple 20¢

orange juice

30¢

apple juice

20¢

He uses four coins.
Draw the coins Kenny uses.

Solve.
Show your work.

2. Brenda has less than 95¢.
After buying a pen, she has 15¢ left.
Which pen does she buy?

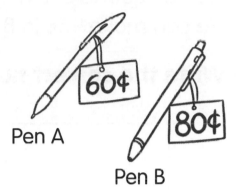

Pen A

Pen B

She buys _____.

3. Keith has more than 70¢ but less than 90¢.
He buys one of the food items.
He has 12¢ left.
Which food does he buy?

orange   pear   bananas
30¢   43¢   60¢

He buys the _____.

Rex wants to buy a balloon for 45¢.
He has quarters, dimes, and nickels.
He can make 45¢ in 8 ways.

Write the correct number of coins.

		45¢	
	Quarter	Dime	Nickel
	1	2	0
4.			
5.			
6.			
7.			
8.			
9.			
10.			

The first way is 1 quarter and 2 dimes.

Name: _____ Date: _____

Chapter Review/Test

Vocabulary

Choose the correct word.

<table>
<tr><td>quarter</td></tr>
<tr><td>less</td></tr>
<tr><td>penny</td></tr>
<tr><td>dime</td></tr>
<tr><td>nickels</td></tr>
</table>

1. A _____ has a value of 10¢.

2. A _____ has a value of 25¢.

3. A dime is _____ than a quarter.

4. A nickel is greater than a _____.

5. 2 _____ have a value of 10¢.

Concepts and Skills

Identify each coin.

6. _____

7. _____

8. _____

9.  _____

Fill in the blanks.

	Exchange	For
10.	1 quarter	_____ dimes, _____ nickel
11.	1 dime	_____ nickels, _____ pennies

Count the money.

12.   is _____¢.

13.

     is _____¢.

Add or subtract.

14.   80¢ + 15¢ = _____

15.   38¢ − 19¢ = _____

Problem Solving
Solve.

16.   Zack has 64¢. He buys a pencil for 25¢.
How much does he have left?

He has _____ left.

17.   Wendy buys a notebook for 52¢,
a bun for 19¢, and a drink for 23¢.
How much does she spend?

She spends _____.

Name: _____ Date: _____

Cumulative Review

for Chapters 18 and 19

Concepts and Skills

Count the number of groups.
Count the number in each group.
Then fill in the blanks.

1.

$6 + 6 + 6 + 6 =$ _____

4 sixes = _____

There are _____ starfishes in all.

2.

$4 + 4 + 4 + 4 =$ _____

4 fours = _____

There are _____ shrimps in all.

Look at the pictures.
Then fill in the blanks.

3.

_____ + _____ + _____ + _____ = _____

_____ fives = _____

4.

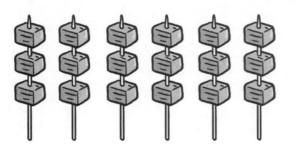

There are _____ pineapple cubes in all.

There are _____ sticks.

There are _____ pineapple cubes in each stick.

Solve.

5.   There are 12 sandwiches.
     They are shared equally by 3 children.

Each child gets _____ sandwiches.

Solve.

6.   There are 16 toy soldiers.
        Jamal packs them equally into 4 boxes.

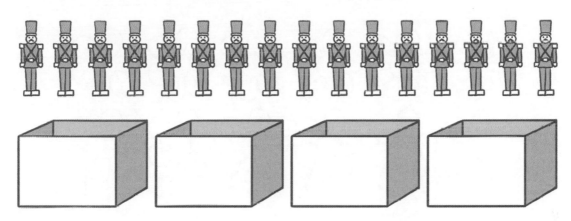

There are _____ toy soldiers in each box.

7.   Timmy puts 6 pillows equally into 3 groups.

Each group has _____ pillows.

8.   There are 9 oranges.
        Circle groups of 3.

There are _____ groups of 3.

© Marshall Cavendish International (Singapore) Private Limited.

Look at the pictures.
Then fill in the blanks.

Maria has 12 flowers.

9.   She puts the flowers equally into 3 vases.

There are _____ flowers in each vase.

10.   She puts 2 flowers in each vase.

She needs _____ vases.

11.   She puts 4 flowers in each vase.

She needs _____ vases.

Write the value.

12.

13.

Fill in the blanks.

14. Find how many of each coin are needed.

_____ dimes _____ nickels

_____ pennies

15. 1 quarter  = _____ nickels

Circle the coins to show the same value.

16. 1 quarter

Circle the coins that are *not* dimes.

17.

Count on to find the value.

18.

_____ ¢

Add.

19.

25¢ + 17¢ = _____ ¢

Complete.

20.

45¢ − 15¢ = _____ ¢

21. Subtract 18¢ from 90¢

_____ − _____ = _____ ¢

Problem Solving
Solve.

22. Draw the least number of coins needed to make 64¢.

End-of-Year Review

Test Prep

Multiple Choice

Fill in the circle next to the correct answer.

1. Which month has less than 31 days?

    (A) January (B) March (C) April (D) October

2. Nina works from Wednesday to the following Monday. How many days does she work?

    (A) 5 (B) 6 (C) 7 (D) 8

3. _____ is the season that comes after Spring.

    (A) Summer (B) Hot (C) Winter (D) Fall

4. The _____ has a value of 5¢.

    (A) penny   (B) dime   (C) quarter   (D) nickel

5. What is the value of the coins?

    (A) 7¢ (B) 19¢ (C) 29¢ (D) 34¢

6. This is the money Shari has.

She buys a red ribbon for 15¢.
How much money does she have left?

(A) 43¢   (B) 53¢   (C) 50¢   (D) 87¢

7. 55¢ + 12¢ = ?

(A) 35¢   (B) 53¢   (C) 67¢   (D) 75¢

8. The third Friday in July is July 17.
What will the fourth Friday be?

(A) July 24   (B) July 22   (C) July 15   (D) August 1

9. 65 comes just before _____.

(A) 55   (B) 64   (C) 66   (D) 75

10.

3 tens and 6 ones is the same as _____.

(A) 8   (B) 11   (C) 36   (D) 83

11. Look at the number pattern.
Which number comes next?
28, 31, 34, 37, 40 _____

(A) 31   (B) 41   (C) 43   (D) 50

12. 10 more than 65 is _____.

(A) 55   (B) 56   (C) 85   (D) 75

13. Add 16 to 57.

(A) 13   (B) 63   (C) 73   (D) 83

14. Find the missing number.
_____ 15, 25, 35, 45

(A) 0   (B) 5   (C) 10   (D) 55

15. Subtract.

$$\begin{array}{r} 4\ \ 5 \\ -\ 3\ \ 6 \\ \hline \end{array}$$

Ⓐ 9　　　Ⓑ 11　　　Ⓒ 19　　　Ⓓ 81

16. Add mentally.

15 + 24 = _____

Ⓐ 7　　　Ⓑ 13　　　Ⓒ 39　　　Ⓓ 35

17.

There are _____ stickers in all.

Ⓐ 6　　　Ⓑ 12　　　Ⓒ 24　　　Ⓓ 30

18. There are _____ squares in the figure.

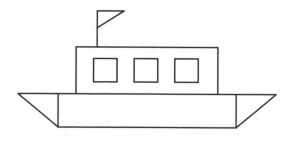

Ⓐ 3　　　Ⓑ 4　　　Ⓒ 5　　　Ⓓ 6

19.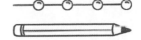

The pencil is about _____ ◦ long.

(A) 8　　　(B) 2　　　(C) 6　　　(D) 4

Short Answer

Write the number in words.

20. 11 _____   **21.** 87 _____

Write the number.

22. fifty-four _____

23. twenty-six _____

Look at the pictures.
Then fill in the blanks.

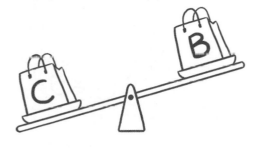
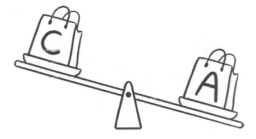

24. Order the bags from lightest to heaviest.

_____   _____   _____
lightest

Look at the picture.
Then fill in the blanks.
Use ○ as 1 unit.

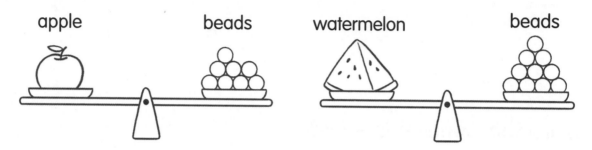

apple   beads   watermelon   beads

25. The weight of the apple is about _____ units.

26. The weight of the watermelon is about _____ units.

27. The _____ is heavier than the _____.

Look at each picture.
Then write the time.

28.

_____

29.

_____

30. Look at the picture.
Then write the number in words.

_____

31. Order the numbers from greatest to least.

| 75 | 41 | 18 | 29 |

_____, _____, _____, _____
   greatest

Circle the two numbers that add up to 4 tens and 4 ones.

32.   24   27   51   30   17

Add the 2nd and 5th numbers.

33.

37	20	19	62	45	83	51
1st						

_____

34. Subtract 6 tens 4 ones
from 8 tens 2 ones.   _____

Name the shape that is shaded.

35.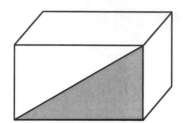

_____

Look at the number line.
Fill in the missing numbers.

36.

45 [ ] [ ] [ ] 65 [ ] 75 80 [ ]

Look at the picture.
Circle the correct word.

37.   Liz   Anita   Ethan

a.   Liz is first   last from the left.

b.   Ethan is in front of   behind Anita.

© Marshall Cavendish International (Singapore) Private Limited.

Extended Response

The picture graph shows the favorite food of 12 children.

38.

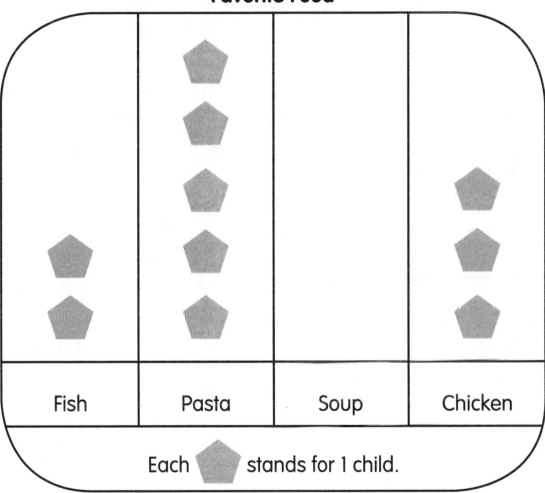

Favorite Food

Each ⬠ stands for 1 child.

Solve.

a. The same number of children named fish and soup as their favorite food.

Draw ⬠ to show the number of children who like soup.

b. _____ is the favorite food for the most children.

Ten families live on the same street.
Every family has one pet.
The picture shows their pets.

Complete the tally chart to show the pet data.
Then answer the questions.

39.

Kinds of Pets		Tally	Number
Hamster			
Cat			
Bird			

a. How many pets are there in all? _____

b. Which pet has the greatest number? _____

Make a bar graph using the data from the tally chart.

c.

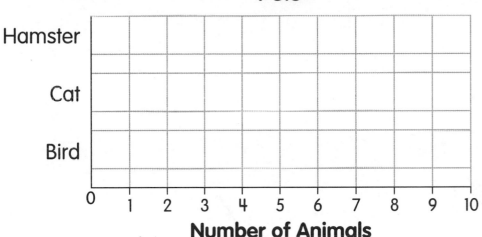

Pets

Kinds of Pets

Hamster

Cat

Bird

Number of Animals

Solve.

40. Sam has 32 marbles
He puts all the marbles in bags.
He puts 4 marbles in each bag.
How many bags does he use?

He uses _____ bags.

BLANK